Self RESCUE

John Cantwell Kiley, M.D., Ph.D.

LOWELL HOUSE
Los Angeles
CONTEMPORARY BOOKS
Chicago

Library of Congress Cataloging-in-Publication Data

Kiley, John Cantwell.
    Self rescue / John Cantwell Kiley.
      p. cm.
    Includes bibliographical references and index.
    ISBN 0-929923-64-2
      1. Self-actualization (Psychology)   2. Conduct of life.
    3. Self (Philosophy)   I. Title.
    BF637.S4K53   1992
    158 ' .1—dc20   92-1077
                                       CIP

Requests for such permissions should be addressed to:

Lowell House
2029 Century Park East, Suite 3290
Los Angeles, CA 90067
Publisher: Jack Artenstein
Executive Vice-President: Nick Clemente
Vice-President/Editor-in-Chief: Janice Gallagher
Director of Marketing: Elizabeth Duell Wood
Manufactured in the United States of America
10 9 8 7 6 5 4 3 2 1

To the Reality of My Brother,
Edward A. Kiley, Jr., Esq.
(1923–1989)
Til we meet again . . .

Also by John Cantwell Kiley:

Einstein and Aquinas: A Rapprochement

Equilibrium: A Guide to Survival

The Heart of a Surgeon: A Study in Self-Rescuing

Perish the Thought: The Stress Connection
(with Herman Lubens, M.D.)

Full Recovery: A Treatise on Survival (forthcoming)

Acknowledgements

I wish to thank Mr. William F. Rickenbacker, who challenged me to write about my devices for coping with my grief upon the death of my father, Edward Augustine Kiley, Sr., and then helped me in the early stages to boil down my ideas and bring my materials into readable form. I am indebted to Professors Joseph Owens and Thomas D. Langan of the University of Toronto, Ralph McInerney of the University of Notre Dame, Raymond L. Forbes of the Naval Postgraduate School, Henry Paolucci of St. John's University, and Narayana Moorty of

7

Monterey Peninsula College for reading the manuscript and suggesting improvements. They saved me from a number of errors but, of course, are not responsible for any that remain. Mr. Travis Selmier and Mr. Joseph Trentin read the manuscript and offered valuable assistance toward publication. Ms. Gay Bostock helped me editorially at various stages of the work and I am most grateful to her for skill, patience and kindness. Mr. John L. Boonshaft played a crucial role in the logistics of bringing this book to publication, and it is unimaginable to me that any writer could have a kinder, more efficient or more knowledgeable ally. Mr. Jed Mattes of International Creative Management in New York and Mr. Howard Portnoy of Carmel, California, helped significantly in bringing the book to market, and I am grateful to both of them. In the long passage to publication I finally fell into the enormously capable hands of Mr. Frederic W. Hills, editor in chief at McGraw-Hill. In him I found combined a rich, quick intelligence, unfailing good humor and uncommon helpfulness which extended generously beyond the editorial. I am deeply in his debt. May the chiefs of such a tribe as his increase! And may their editorial assistants: I speak of Ms. Mary Moran, a rare and beautiful woman snatched up recently in holy matrimony by a lucky man. I wish to acknowledge my debt to Professor William Ernest Carlo, "a verray parfit, gentil knight," for his philosophic gifts to me through thirty years as friend and teacher. Though he is deceased, I will not call him "late": his reality to me remains present and undiminished. My final debt is to my father, equally very much alive to me, whose passing prompted this work and whose whole life was an embodiment of courage and truth. This book exists in the first place only because of his unquenchable love for me.

10

Contents

11

Introduction

WELL, you won't soon read another book like this one.

This is the very least that can be promised for a self-help book that assimilates psychology to ontology—a practical manual with a metaphysical surprise ending. The ending can't very well be "given away," even if one would: the controversial conclusion grows too intimately out of what precedes it. And to prescind it from its context of applied insights would perhaps tempt the reader to the precipitate inference that the author is nuts.

But John Kiley is crazy like a fox. Or perhaps it would be better to say, like an ox—the Dumb Ox, as some college boys of the 1240s dubbed Thomas Aquinas. *Self-Rescue* is beholden to Aquinas, Shakespeare, Chesterton (who, by the way, wrote a book about Aquinas called *The Dumb Ox*), and assorted Eastern sages rather than to Freud or B. F. Skinner. It eschews familiar methods of stimulation, manipulation, and analysis: its emphasis is on harmony with "the nourishing and sustaining things" and avoiding absorption in "the lethal thoughts." If he demands courage of the reader, he also reminds him serenely that the resources of courage are simply there, for whoever truly desires them. One thinks of the pianist Paderewski, who was once complimented by an effusive lady admirer on his incredible patience. "I have no more patience, Madam, than anyone else," he replied. "I merely use mine." Likewise, Kiley would remind you, you have no less fortitude than the saints: you merely have to deploy it.

John Kiley is a towering, red-bearded leprechaun of a man who has probably never in his life done anything expectedly. Readers of *National Review* know him as Johannes Eff, sublime light versifier, who has for twenty years regaled them with epigram and epic, a sort of Ogden Nash *cum* Maritain. He has been, during most of that time, a professor of philosophy, of a whimsical turn to be sure—Maritain *cum* Nash—but all the more popular and fruitful as a teacher for that. He has written political speeches (he specializes in lost causes, both out of gallantry and conviction). For the last five years he has been a close student of theology. What next?

Why this, psychology—or rather "clinical philosophy," which, he tells us at the outset, "is more concerned with healing the being (ontiatry) than with healing the psyche (psychiatry, psychoanalysis, behavioral psychology)." What we need is to face the worst, to see how rich we remain when we think we have "lost everything," rich in the deepest human capacities for survival and joy. He speaks of the great devastations of the soul—grief, remorse, despair—with the eloquence of perfect precision. He knows the repose of soul that comes of acknowledging one's own smallness. Of all this he speaks without a syllable of the oppressive jargon of the established psychologies.

But I would like to enter a small reservation. Namely, that he is wrong. This may seem a petty point in an age when Hans Kung is permitted to swing from the Vatican chandeliers; but it must be said. What he is wrong about is this: "The existence of everything is included in the divine existence. This means that absolutely everything is God." That, if he will permit me between the covers of his own book, is false, and it *matters* that it is false. It means that the Creator cannot create. A spider can spin a web, and the web is distinct from the spider; a feeble image of creation, but there it is. To say that God can only produce more of himself is to say that he is less than the spider. It would be better to say that there is no God than that everything is God, because atheism is still an affirmation that it really makes a difference what exists. Even materialism is a kind of brute genuflection before being. But pantheism is an idiocy; an idiocy in the literal etymological sense of a secession from the objective and public world of reality, where our privacies intersect—a shrinking up into the ego. Montaigne jibed that man, who cannot even make a worm, will yet make gods by the dozens. Pantheism makes a god who cannot even create a worm, because he is a worm. I will believe in nothing less exalted than a God who could make a Jack Kiley.

But there is this to be said for his pantheism, that unlike the pantheisms of the East and of Spinoza, it is not a theology of exhaustion. It is an attempt to express adequately his sense of the abundance of things, and their relatedness (at the expense, it is true, of their distinctness). The only weakness of his formulations is that in reminding us that few of the things that agitate us are important, they suggest that nothing at all is important. "In the absolute sense," he concedes, "I am forced to say that nothing new is ever really happening." But we have it on good authority that Creation and

Redemption are always happening: "Behold, I make all things new." The best earnest of his healthy sense of the Lord's bounty is his evident reluctance—he is "forced"—to say that nothing is new. It is not a position he embraces: it is one he is reduced to.

So ignore the abstractions. Cleave to the practical wisdom of this book. It has found the contemporary idiom for an older consolation:

"The Lord is my shepherd: I shall not want."

WILLIAM F. BUCKLEY, JR.

To The Reader

What you are about to read is concerned more with healing the being (using what I term "ontiatry") than with healing the psyche (using psychiatry, psychoanalysis, behavioral psychology, etc.). In this book there is a conscious shift from psychology to ontology (the study of being) or, as it might be viewed, from clinical psychology to clinical philosophy. Those who realize that philosophy is historically the parent discipline will not be shocked by such an approach.

The reader is reminded that the book was written developmentally and therefore should be read, at least the first time, as a totality. The chapters, it is hoped, stand on their own but at the same time are embedded in a larger background and community of ideas and proposals.

J. K.

And God-appointed Berkeley that proved all things a
   dream;
That this pragmatical, preposterous pig of a world, its farrow
   that so solid seem,
Must vanish on the instant if the mind but change its
   theme.
                        William Butler Yeats

Prologue—
The Logic of
Self Rescue

YOU ASK: What is this book all about? It is about self-rescue theory and a self-rescue program, one that can liberate you right now, this instant, from the often tragic consequences of waiting for an outside rescue that may never come. Its range is as wide as the afflictions that man generates within himself: anxiety, grief, remorse, loneliness, desperation, boredom and many more. Few of us are entirely free from one or another of them.

The key to mental health is the timely use of the art of self-rescue. It is, after all, the self who gets the first signals of distress, who is first on the scene. The self is also the victim, and, at the same time, its own best and most devoted ally. Accordingly, the self should be adequate to its own needs, be able to capitalize on its physical self-presence, self-involvement and primary awareness of distress.

The one big mistake is waiting to have your rescue carried out for you. By your wife or husband, by your parents, friends or clergyman, by your lawyer, accountant, analyst, psychiatrist or guru, by anyone. They are not here now. When you need them most, now, they are out to lunch. Not only that, but some of them are very expensive.

The irony is they can't or won't help you anyway. Except in various superficial ways.

Who you need is you. You, your best friend, closest ally, greatest sympathizer, most sincere admirer and flatterer, most trusted confidant—and perhaps just as often your most savage critic. You, where it hurts, where it's lonely and chaotic, full of worries and unwelcome surprises. The victim needs himself. The one in need of rescue must undertake it himself in behalf of himself.

Why not? What do all those others have compared to *your* self-proximity, self-interest, self-involvement and self-knowledge? You are the best expert on yourself; the doctor has to ask *you* where it hurts and how much. To you, you are number one, politely deny it though you may, and the minute that you forget it, *you* bear the chief consequences and nobody else.

That is what this book is about: a theory and practice of rescuing yourself immediately from anguish and unhappiness.

The basic reason for an *immediate* rescue is this: now is really where it's at, where everyone and everything is. (If this is not evident now, I hope the book will make it so.) The even more basic reason is that the *now* is *all* there is. The art of self-rescue is the art of living in the *now*. It is also the art of being free, the *now* being the natural habitat of the free being. The true slave cannot rescue himself, nor can the dreamer, for, being outside the *now*, each is denied access to the only resources which will rescue him.

Consider some characteristics of the *now*:

The *now* is punctual. It comes with predictable regularity. It never fails to arrive, promptly, like some well-run train.

The *now* is neutral. It does not resist insertion of any content, however trivial, however important.

The *now* is short-lived. It appears and just as quickly disappears. However long awaited, it stays but an instant and is gone.

The *now* is inexorable. It proceeds forward, without cease, subject to no resistance; it is unwearying, utterly irrepressible.

Finally, but most important, the *now* is unique. Without this uniqueness, there would be no breaking with the past, no future to grow into, no present in which to realize yourself. Your claim to freedom would be illusory, a dream-act in which nothing of real significance ever happens.

Uniqueness fully allows for the important ways in which a present *now* will resemble a past *now* and a future *now*, for in those certain ways each *now* is like all other *nows*, just as things of the same kind—apples, houses, and rainstorms—resemble each other. *But, unless the now is seen as a fresh new moment bound to no past and undetermined toward any future, there is no basis for the belief in the possibility of acting freely in any particular now.* Without the liberation that the sense of the unique and untrammeled *now* bestows on your consciousness, all your acts would be but the rigidly predetermined gestures of a string-bound puppet.

There is a moment in the now when you see a field of choices open to you. It may be the smallest possible field, calling for either a simple yes ("I will take this person for my mate") or a simple no ("I will not"), for example. In that moment, in that new, unique and unbound now, you hold yourself in freedom before the pull of alternatives.

The free act, then, happens in the *now*; the *now* is the only soil in which it can come to be.

This is only because the *now* is a unique moment unconnected to any past or to any future.

The *now* is where it's at. You want relief *now*. Release, understanding, remedies, solutions—*now*. That is what this book is all about. To show you how to have them *now*. All by yourself.

1
How to Get Out of a Snowbank

All religion is concerned to overcome fear. The maxim of illusory religion runs: "Fear not; trust in God and He will see that none of the things you fear will happen to you." That of real religion on the contrary is: "Fear not; the things that you are afraid of are quite likely to happen to you, but they are nothing to be afraid of."
          John MacMurray

SOME years ago a national magazine printed a true story about a man who, while skiing in the mountains of Switzerland, fell into a deep snowbank and disappeared from sight. The tip of one of his ski poles, which bore a tiny red flag, protruded from the bank and was seen by a member of the search party just as it was about to abandon the search after several days and nights.

Imagine yourself, if you can stand the vicarious terror, in that man's predicament. If rescued, would you emerge the same person who started out on skis that bright, sunny morning, carefree in the snowy mountains? How would you have borne the simple thought, as you lay there fully conscious and unhurt, scarcely able to move a finger, so impacted by the snow all about you that you may be, indeed are, beyond help and that the snowbank will now become your grave? And that you must die in it, slowly, by starvation, while utterly alone, unable to help yourself, your screams muffled by the deep tomb of snow you occupy. The thought of it so terrifying, how could you endure the experience?

And yet, had you been that man, you would have had to endure it. You would be in a situation which would be impervious to any change of mind or plans, unalterably real.

Ah, you say, if you were in that predicament, you would panic, become hysterical, scream, cry. But when all screamed out, you are still in the snowbank, not an inch nearer to rescue. Screaming, having a fit, gets you exactly... nowhere.

Well, then, you would kill yourself? But you are impacted and can only wiggle a finger or two, nothing more. How will you do it? By holding your breath? You will hold it until it hurts too much, then you will be happy to breathe again. Indeed, the snow is porous and the air is plentiful.

Mercifully, you would soon freeze to death? No, you are, if anything, too warm. The sun's rays dimly reach you during the day and at night the snow insulates you from the mountain cold like the warmest of blankets.

You would let yourself die of thirst before you would swallow any snow? Such a death would be more painful than starving to death and the temptation to slake your thirst with a mouthful of snow would be irresistible and defeat your purpose.

You would think of some way out? What? Here is a situation where thinking will do you absolutely no good. It is a unique situation.

But it is unique for another reason, too. You are now in a situation where thinking will harm you, terrify, derange and madden you. Thinking will galvanize you to action, to do something, to undertake this operation or that, to go somewhere. But you have nothing to do but panic, nowhere to go but up your own brainstem. Thinking will keep you richly and continuously informed on your mortal peril. And your helplessness. Thinking will pump melodrama into your brain, flood you with frustration, anger, fear, regret, self-pity, rebellion, grief, all in mind-blowing waves. Thinking will convulse your soul with alarm, stalk you with terror, raise you up for a brief instant, then hurl you down to a bottomless pit of abandonment and despair. But if you are lucky, rather, blessed with the grace to realize it, you may soon come to recognize that your first and cruelest enemy is . . . thinking.

All your life until now you thought that thinking was an unassailable good. Ah, how clever you had become at it! How you could think out solutions to all your problems! How skillfully you could rationalize actions! Did *this* interfere? Thought soon removed it. Did *that* annoy? How brilliant of you to think of the remedy! Was it marriage, a business contract, some annoying task or responsibility? Thinking soon extricated you. Or so it seemed. In any case, what did not work out was not the fault of thinking, but of thinking badly. Shoddy thinking. Fuzzy thinking. Not thinking it through. Not giving it enough thought.

Besides, thinking can sustain hope. It can also seize control and prompt an act of suicide. Suicide, however, is an academic matter for you. Such thoughts are beyond your physical power to implement. No, you will have to be "rescued" in some other way. Some other way that you, yourself, must invent at once.

But what is it you most need to be rescued from? From death? You are in no immediate danger of dying. Right now you are safer than in a car on the highway. From what, then? You need to be rescued from terror. Panic. Hysteria.

When you are missed, people skilled in rescue work will come looking for you. This can be of some comfort to you. But there is more. Even if these searchers, unable to find you in reasonable time, tire of looking and give up the search, you need not feel abandoned.

To avoid being the living, conscious site of

unspeakable terror, you must widen at once your definition of abandonment. Consider. Were you to be truly abandoned, abandoned in the absolute sense, you would have an infinity of years ahead of you in your white limbo, suspended there in that eternal home of snow, growing no weaker, progressing toward no conclusion, utterly unnoticed by the cosmos. Such, mercifully, is not your fate. While in no immediate danger of death, you will discover death to be your prompt and efficient "backup rescuer," should society fail you. Death, unlike your well-meaning but fallible human fellows, will not fail you. And it will rescue you at the appropriate moment, when your real being has abandoned all hope at the cellular level. Then, as you are carried gently into a benign and delicious coma, death will lift you out of the snow and end your confinement. Thus your certain deliverance. You need only wait.

Clearly, you are not one-who-*only*-waits. You are one-who-waits-with-absolute-faith in your final deliverance. You have rid yourself of the narrow concept of social rescue-as-ultimate and supplied yourself with a consciousness to ride out the sense of abandonment and the terror that is its awful child. You do not merely *hope* to be rescued, provided this or that bit of luck holds, you have infallible *knowledge* of your coming rescue.

Oh, such a rescue as you know will happen may not recommend itself to your conventional thought, or fit in at all with your personal wishes and preferences, but reality is forcing you to give up such forms of social conditioning. You are in the process of discovering at last what has always been true but obscured by thought, *that the real order of things is the ultimate arbiter of what will be.* Like it or not, accept it or not, you are now hidden in a real snowbank in desolate mountainous wastes. You are being educated, bluntly, as to the way the world really is. You are being taught at the very fountainhead of being, and what you are learning goes by the holy word, Wisdom.

Your consciousness is now expanded beyond thought. And since it is, such thoughts that come to you from your social past no longer carry their former weight. You let them come and you watch them go, like lights from passing cars slanting across your night ceiling. You are no longer their solemn and attentive keeper, but a kind of bemused observer on the sidelines. You see them now as mere visitors rather than residents, as transients on their way to somewhere else.

Much of the time your mind is, in fact, empty of thought. This is not because you are asleep or in some vague reverie, but because you are in immediate and continuous touch with yourself, your body, the enclosing world of snow around you. While the background of your consciousness is inhabited by an unshakable faith in your rescue after a short wait, the forefront of your consciousness now sees what there is to see, hears what can be heard, touches, smells and tastes what is available to it. Your consciousness is in a state of supple alertness. If your would-be rescuer passes within the extreme radius of your hearing—which is much greater to a focused consciousness—you will be ready with your own signal. Furthermore, you will not have spent your voice in mindless screaming.

Meanwhile, the real things with which you are in contact will nourish you and keep you company. You will be brought into a new intimacy with yourself and come to perceive your reality directly, the veil of social role-playing and cultural conditioning stripped away. You will realize that all your life you have been a stranger to yourself. You will see that you are none of the things you thought you were, but rather something vastly richer and more real, a realization that will warm you and somehow compensate you for what you have lost. You will be taught many primary lessons because now reality has a chance to get past the outer ego-wall that has been building around you since your birth. It can now penetrate to your full and deepest consciousness.

At times you will fall gently asleep, narcotized by the thing acting on your consciousness. You will not have terrible nightmares and will wake up instantly should any signal reach you from the outside. You are one-who-waits-for-whatever-is-to-happen. You have intuitive faith in the unquenchable benignity of the cosmos. You are occupying religiously the place that the universe, for its own reasons, has assigned you. Your waiting-in-the-*now* in this existential manner is your living prayer, and, since the whole universe is alive with one great cohering life, your prayer is being heard.

2

How to Survive
a Tragedy

All my pretty ones?
Did you say all? O Hellkite! All?
What, all my pretty chickens and their dam
At one fell swoop.
> *Macduff*, MACBETH,
> Act 4, scene 3

*T*HE telephone rings. You put down the Saturday afternoon paper and answer it.

"Hello, is this Mr. Smith?"

"Yes, it is."

"This is Dr. Brown at Community Hospital."

Panic. Your heart races. The phone suddenly begins to shake in your hand. Fear. Images of disaster flash through your brain.

"What is it?" You blurt out the words in terror.

"There has been a traffic accident involving

your family. Come to the emergency room at once. Community Hospital, Twelfth and Main."

You want to know the worst, the very worst. Right now. No, not right now. Later. Tomorrow. Never.

"What happened. Doctor? Tell me for God's sake!"

"Please come at once. I will see you here."

"Okay, I'm leaving now." You put down the phone. The room swims before your eyes. You lean against the wall. Your heart is slamming against your chest and your breathing comes in gasps. You find the closet, grab your jacket, fumble for the keys in the pocket and rush to your car. You drive the thirty blocks to the hospital. Of the ride itself you remember nothing.

At the hospital you learn the worst thing imaginable: your wife and all your children have been killed. They died instantly in a head-on crash with a dump truck. The truck driver, who was only slightly injured, said his brakes failed and when he tried to stop the truck went out of control and shot across the highway barrier. The police tell you this. They are holding the man in custody.

If he were not in custody, in your grief, your rage, you would kill him. You would tear him apart with your hands. Him and his whole family. Him and his whole family and God too. Why? Why? Tears well up and run down your cheeks into your mouth. The doctor offers you a sedative. No. The nurses hover in the background, looking awkward, and one of them steps forward and says something consoling. Now a priest arrives and sits by your side, takes your hand and holds it. What can he say? He says nothing. Just sits there with you. You are utterly alone. Desolated. Abandoned. Cut down. The tears are hot, sting your cheeks, drip from your chin onto your hands. No, you will not believe it. It could not have happened. Not to Aimee. Not to Billy and Mickey and little Sarah. No.

But it has happened. To Aimee, to Billy, to Mickey, to Sarah. And to you. Your loved ones have been taken from you. In one fell swoop. Just as Shakespeare imagined it. All your pretty chickens. All! All!

When sorrows come, they come not single spies,
But in battalions.[1]

How will you bear it? Shakespeare knows how you suffer: "My grief lies onward, and my joy behind."[2] He tells you, king or not, how you are going to feel:

Grief fills the room of my absent child
Lies in his bed, walks up and down with me,
Puts on his pretty looks, repeats his words,
Remembers me of all his gracious parts,
Stuffs out his vacant garments with his form.[3]

It is not that you are totally unready for this grief, totally unprepared. Of course you read the newspapers, the history books. You are conversant with the facts of the human condition, the universal human coming-to-grief. Yet always what you knew and read about were the tragedies of others—strangers slain in battle, unknown victims of flood and famine, anonymous fatalities of airplane crashes. You knew that nobody was forever safe from chance, from accident, from their own mortality. You rejoiced that your loved ones were untouched even as tragedy all around you hedged your joy and mocked your small defenses.

You were prepared but you were not prepared. Not for this, not for real loss, real grief. For the *thought* of losing Aimee, yes. But not for *really* losing her. Shakespeare, once more, with poor dead Cordelia:

> LEAR. And my poor fool is hanged! No, no, no life!
> Why should a dog, a horse, a rat, have life
> And thou no breath at all? Thou'lt come no more,
> Never, never, never, never, never![4]

Tragedy has come down from the stage where for years you watched it, engrossed. As a spectator. It has come to you in your very seat and put the real dagger in your heart. This is not the grief you bought at the box-office window, relieved as it was between the acts and by the final curtain. No. That was no preparation for this grief, this sickness in your soul, this mauling and devouring, this living murder of you even while you still live.

Shakespeare provided you with models for

tragedy, abundantly so, and let you see grief spread on a wide canvas. He did you this service. Let you play at grieving. But it was insufficient preparation, after all.

You are cried out now, beyond tears, alone. Your family has been lowered into the earth, your heart buried with them. Relatives and friends, counselors at grief, have all done what little they could for you. It is not their fault that words fall on you like lead slugs on a stoop. What are words, after all, to the happy busy noises in the kitchen, the beds filled with three small beauties in their plump sleep, the quick demand—"Daddy, look at this"—the walks, the rides, the frets, the fun, the falls, the laughs, the tears, a wife at your side, the touches in the night, the life, the blessed, blessed life and lives. . . . Gone. Gone. Utterly gone.

You must go on? All say you must go on. But why must you? Give one good reason, one will be enough, why you must go on.

Go on? For what, you ask. Why go on? How? It comes down finally to this: How?

The how of going on is in your heart. In its beating, in its pumping blood to you. It is in your ribs, your spleen, your hair, your legs, your hands. Look at your hands. They persist, do they not? Their shaking has stopped. They are the old familiar hands you had before, are they not? Touch them. Touch your hands. Can you feel them? They are the way you will go on. They are the way of your eyes, ears, nose and tongue. These, good servants, faithful and loyal friends, will lead you out of the darkness of your misery and grief. They will take you to the blue sky, the smell of lilacs, the sound of birds, the taste of apple. They, if you let them, will take you from your mind where madness breeds, where poisons brew their fatal doses to your heart, your very will to live, where tortured thoughts of what you had and lost lie to ambush you and pull you down to miseries more terrible than all your present grief.

The how of going on, you discover, must be in things—it cannot be in your thoughts, for they offer only desolation and despair. You must surround yourself with things, and as you turn to this task, you discover it is not difficult, since they are all around you already. You must gather these things to yourself, just as they are. And not things which act on you as starting points for thought, for example, of reveries about what was or might have been. Rather things in themselves, things in their simple being, beauty, sturdiness, softness, shape, color. These, properly experienced (and what is proper to you is not proper for someone else untouched by your losses and sadness), will anchor you in the *now* and defend you from the thoughts which would keep you continuously informed about your tragedy and bring home, in wave after wave of consciousness, your desolation and misery.

And what is the good of unreconciled grieving? What is the good of inviting the birds of sorrow, as the ancient Chinese proverb asks, to come nest in your very hair, called down from their flight above you? Is it not wiser to let time begin at once its work of repair and healing by growing a tissue of forgetfulness over your wound?

You need do nothing more than stay in continuous touch with the things that surround you. You must realize that your mortal enemy is not your loss but your *thought* about your loss. You must learn to defend yourself like an expert. And this ability is entirely within your power, if you understand what must be done—and persist at it through discouragement and seeming defeat. Expect stumblings, expect lapses, particularly at first, but know that expertness here will come much quicker to you than in some other "unnatural" activity, such as golf or chess. Remember: Your allies are everywhere in the things that exist in your immediate world. These allies come in every size and shape, color and texture. The water in your faucet will not only quench your thirst but defend you from your thoughts if you let it. The trees and sky through your window can fill your consciousness, in any moment you choose, with their quiet healing presence. The real world, in other words, will rescue you from grief, if you allow it to enter your consciousness.

But your efforts toward inner peace, toward the preservation of your very sanity and life, must be carried out with a double strategy. Even as you use your five senses to stay in the *now* of real time by orienting your "foreground consciousness" to things, you will need a suitable "background consciousness" for more general support.* Ideally, the most suitable background consciousness is the one that enables you to heal the quickest and with the smallest scars. And this is one by which you understand the ultimately benign nature of the cosmic drama in which all beings are involved. The great, holy personages of the world religions assure us that what on the human plane is experienced as a loss or tragedy is really not so at all, but only seems so, and that everything will turn out right in the end.

Believing this, or better, understanding it, gives you a background consciousness to cope with your grief most effectively. This is because it is an orientation to the real order of the whole universe in its truest and most real character. It is, in

---

*The "foreground" is that part of your consciousness which attends to the business of coping moment by moment with the changing physical circumstances of your life, as when driving a car, eating a meal, etc. The "background" is concerned with more general matters, for example, when driving, with the purpose of the drive, the values of caution, the limitations of time, etc., or when eating, with the questions of cost, health, taste, etc., and, while living, with the general goals of avoiding pain and achieving happiness. Personal reflection on the workings of your consciousness will show, particularly when some concrete action is being performed, the truth of this division of your consciousness into a "foreground" part that attends to details of an action, and a "background" part that is concerned with the larger matters of when, where, why, how and if.

fact, religion according to its meaning of "connection." With such a consciousness the death and loss of your loved ones can begin to make "sense" because the event is lifted off the purely human plane of human accident and error to the cosmic or divine plane where all things cohere, are united and in full reconciliation with reality itself. To put it simply, you will have the wisdom to accept what is *because it is*, as contrasted with the foolishness that resists such an acceptance and is consumed in trying to hold on to what is not.

Your grief now, while still a true grief, has been cut down to bearable proportions. It will be the work of the chapters that follow to show in greater depth and detail how it can be that with the infinite resources of the world to support you and your trust in the basic love and care of the world for itself, your peace will be restored to you.

3

How to Keep from Wounding Yourself

I always keep a supply of stimulants on hand in case I meet a snake, which I also keep on hand.
                              W.C. Fields

*T*HERE was a farmer who one day lost his hand in a threshing machine. He blacked out at once and upon regaining consciousness observed a bloody stump where his right hand used to be. He fell silent, fighting back tears. Then he roused himself and asked where his hand was. "We buried it, Pa," said one of his sons quietly. "Go dig it up and bring it to me," commanded the farmer. The son quickly returned with the severed hand and placed it in his father's lap. The man looked at it for a long while, then picked it

up with his remaining hand and fondled it lov-
ingly. "I'm going to miss you, old friend," he
sighed. "I didn't really appreciate you when I had
you, but I do now, now that I've lost you, now
when it's too late."

The farmer's remark is poignant, and it points
up a very important truth about human happiness:
Possessing a thing is never as good as being
deprived of it is bad. In order to appreciate what
we have, we must experience in some way, real or
imaginary, the loss of it. Yet, understandably,
humans do not normally seek out real losses, or
comfortably conjure up imaginary ones. It is a
human predicament: Humans recoil from losses,
yet without them there is no vantage point from
which to savor what one has.

Clearly the possession by the farmer of two
hands was good—we are considering at this point
his *awareness* of what he had, his savoring of it. No
doubt he found his hand supremely useful, but in a
busy life he never took the time to focus on just
how useful, how marvelous it was. Now its loss has
provided him with that focus, but only when there
is no hand left to appreciate.

It would be interesting to follow the remaining years of that farmer, to learn how he bore his
loss, to inquire whether his accident was a one-
time affair in his life—something with which he
quickly came to terms—or whether it was the
beginning of a continuing process of self-wound-

ing, of sorrowing for his hand, of reliving the accident, of blaming, of protesting, of self-pitying.

Self-wounding. The urge to chastise, to punish the self for its blunders, to hold the self responsible for its faults, its errors, its misadventures. It is a deep and strange urge which I have and you have, an urge which, unless checked, can end disastrously for us.

It is clear that the best, the healthiest reaction for the farmer to his accident would have been to bury all regret, all sense of loss, all self-pity with his hand, to walk away mentally from the event and never look back. In so doing he would have been cutting his losses to a minimum. His loss would have been limited to his hand—bad enough, it is true, but not worsened by time wasted "minding" his loss, dead time serving only to intensify the accident by giving it a time-reach it didn't of itself possess—all without bringing back his hand.

The urge to wound oneself is bound up with the urge to relive a previous happy state, to regain an earlier possession. Yet if the farmer (you or I in similar circumstances) was not to be a victim of this urge to wound himself, this is precisely what he would not have done. He needed to bury not just his hand, but the memory of his hand as well, a far more important burial to his peace and future happiness.

The urge to wound oneself seldom takes the

direct form. We rarely intend a self-wounding. Its occurrence is a side-effect. We are in pursuit of our happiness as we perceive it and are often surprised and dismayed when trauma rather than happiness results. At such times we have blundered, we have taken a road that leads in the wrong direction, and so long as we stay on that road the results are predictable: sadness, frustration, disappointment. Getting off that road is our immediate task.

It is not that you or I set out to wound ourselves but rather that we choose, with more freedom than we realize, to produce within ourselves those mental states which, once constituted, produce their inevitable result.

It would have been psychologically impossible for the farmer to remember the hand he lost and not be saddened by that remembrance. You cannot travel the road that takes you back mentally to better times and climes without involving yourself in a journey of sadness. And if your goal is peace and contentment, you must stay off that road. You must not produce those states of consciousness which disturb you.

And what of the subsequent years of our farmer? He missed his hand for the rest of his life but, happily for him, he missed it only when two hands would have better turned the tractor, wielded a pitchfork, carved a turkey. After sixty years of two-handed life, such reminders were perhaps inescapable. But he was a wise if not entirely lucky man, for he saw what he must do to avoid ending up not only pitied but self-pitying. He would have to accept his loss, which for him meant making believe that he was born with one hand while being grateful that for sixty years he had the use of two. He had been wounded in an accident. It had happened to him and there was no way he could undo it. But there was nothing about that accident which required him to add to the injury by wounding himself further. He saw this clearly. And with his one good hand he pursued a productive life. What he already knew, now we must learn: how to cut short the long reach that accidents can have in our lives and how to use all our finite resources of time for happy and fruitful living.

4

How to Live
With Remorse

The agenbite of inwit . . .
James Joyce, "FINNEGAN'S WAKE"

YOU have done what you should not have done; not done what you should have. When this thought occurs to you, your peace is at once destroyed. It is the wound that will not heal.

You have piled up great wealth and authority, surrounded yourself with sincere admirers, busied yourself with projects that are important, praiseworthy and noble, kept the great gong of pleasure and distraction resounding in your life. Yet, despite all you have done and are willing to do to leave behind forever that which you should not have done or that which you did not do, unhappiness walks beside you like an evil ghost.

> One need not be a Chamber—to be Haunted—
> One need not be a House—
> The Brain has corridors—surpassing
> Material Place—[1]

It is too late for that which you should not have done, for that which you did, to be rewritten. It is too late to understand now at last that there is a primal, unconditioned law written on your heart that you cannot choose the way that you know is wrong, inferior to or less perfect than some other way, with impunity.

And what is the consequence of doing what you ought not to do? It is a feeling of guilt, a guilt that grows spontaneously and irresistibly as a weed from the soil of a failed opportunity. And that weed, once sprung, will produce with time's passage its bitter fruit whose name is . . . remorse.

Remorse, then, is not some capricious and uncaused state, unconnected to some past act. It is the lingering aftereffect of a self-inflicted wounding of your moral being or conscience which carries with it a lifelong craving to make amends by rectifying or reconstituting the past.

But there is no way to rectify or reconstitute the past. In the words of Fitzgerald's *Rubaiyat*,

> The Moving Finger writes; and having writ,
> Moves on: nor all your Piety nor Wit
> Shall lure it back to cancel half a Line
> Nor all your tears wash out a Word of it.[2]

Remorse is the pitiless, untiring dog pack that keeps bringing down the lovely leaping gazelle of your open-plained happiness. And what of that pursuing dog pack, you ask. Will it never tire of hounding me, of biting through my heart even as I am in the very act of savoring the sweet bouquet of hard-won happiness? How long must I pay for what I once did, for what I once failed to do, with this blood money of remorse, this heavy specie of sorrow engraved with the *ecce homo* of my own face? Must I keep repeating without relief the poet's dirge,

> For of all sad words of tongue and pen,
> The saddest are these: "It might have been!"[3]

It is here that the art of self-rescue is most critically tested. Here on that familiar terrain where everyone does almost daily battle with his might-have-beens. Here, whether you are bravely facing the old enemy or frantically running from him into some feeble distraction, remorse marches against your bows and arrows with howitzers and tanks. How can you win not just a truce from this pain, primal in the whole catalogue of human pain, but a permanent peace?

The self-rescue art is not the art of romantic visualization. Its goal is not peace achieved by some "final victory" in which the enemy is slain once and for all. Indeed, in the case of remorse, the battle was moral, fought previously and lost. The enemy occupies the brain, a creature of memory, rather than some objectively real terrain. What the art of self-rescue aims at is setting up an adequate defense against this enemy of your peace so that peace can be sued-for unilaterally and at your own discretion and pleasure. The art makes no promise or pretense of bringing to your consciousness a perfect and uninterrupted peace. It promises only to provide peace in any given *now*.

Applied concretely to the problem of remorse, the art of self-rescue involves the twofold adjustment of your consciousness in both its background and foreground aspects.

In its background, the consciousness is deeply aware that all past events, unexceptionally, have a past-reality status; that is; they are wholly dependent for their reality upon an exercise of memory. In addition, the self-rescue consciousness has a background realization that the problem of coping with the pain of remorse is, given the nature of time, never long-range but always a matter of what occurs in each lived *now*. There is the realization that remorse is a pain you can quite easily bear precisely because you no longer can be ambushed by it. You are now able to choose the time and place of confrontation. It is you who, in your own time, open the gates of your internal city for a light skirmish within and who can close the gates again at will, expelling your enemy.

You ask: Why, if this is so, would I deliberately open my gates to needless pain and suffering? The answer is, because the pain teaches you.

You learn continually through that voice from your past about the moral nature of reality. You must, therefore, welcome such instruction into your life, even as you protect yourself against its power. For remorse has the power to destroy as well as instruct.

The foreground consciousness works within the master plan or framework set by the background consciousness, with special work to do within that framework. If the latter is the philosopher of your life, the foreground consciousness is the engineer. It is the operational or tactical side of consciousness. It is here that your moment-to-moment controls are stationed; it is here the pieces of your time-units are each laid down to form the whole mosaic of your life.

The sense faculties work effectively only when they are in focus. The eye does not really see, except in some vague way, unless directed to some concrete object. This is also true of the organs of hearing, touching, smelling and tasting. Such organs need to be directed to their proper objects by consciousness. It is the foreground consciousness that does this.

The foreground consciousness has the vital task, then, of focusing the sense faculties, which activates their powers. But, for what reason? Speaking generally, for getting you into touch with the real world of things. In particular, as in the case of remorse, for the purpose of dealing with remorse aggressively. By aggressively, I mean in a way that puts you in control of the pain of remorse and enables you to decide when it will be allowed to reach your consciousness.

One of the great axiomatic truths of the self-rescue art is this: *Full sensory awareness of the thing and preoccupation with thought cannot be simultaneously maintained by consciousness:* One state precludes the other. You can readily demonstrate this simple truth to yourself in the following way. Right now think of an elephant. Imagine it as clearly as you can. Then, quickly, listen to the noise of a passing car, or touch the back of your hand. Instantly the thought and image you were producing vanished from your consciousness. You can of course reproduce the mental impression of the elephant (symbolizing here any and all mental states) again at will, but only if you first turn away from sense contact with the thing that is holding your attention. And the significance of this fact of consciousness in regard to the pain of remorse is clear: *When your consciousness is occupied with the sense experience of the thing, the gates of your own city are closed to remorse; you are safe, secure and at peace within.*

The self-rescue art thus passes the crucial test of effectiveness against remorse, that common thief and enemy of human happiness.

5

How to Avoid Suicide

I would never belong to any country club that would have me as a member.
    Groucho Marx

YOU are stymied completely. You have been over the scenario countless times in your head searching for a way out, an escape route, from the morass that grips you, but there is no way out, no way that you can find, and you are sure no one else can find. It is hopeless. You are utterly boxed in, immured in your profound predicament —as we said, completely stymied.

Completely? Oh, there is one way out and there are no doubt lots of people for whom that way out was always part of some theoretical game-plan, ready to be implemented "if things got too bad." For you Hamlet's escape (taking arms against a sea of troubles and evading them, by suicide) was never part of your strategy. You knew suicide happened, but such was your upbringing, such your ethical postulates, such your lust for living, that it always horrified you. You recoiled from it totally. It occupied no part of your consciousness, because you fiercely denied it access, like some ferocious Tibetan dog guarding day and night his master's courtyard.

Now you are in the thick of an intolerable situation from which you perceive there is no conceivable escape. Your endless review of the situation has not only totally convinced you of the impossibility of an acceptable extrication but has begun to weary and nauseate you with its useless labor. Suddenly the forbidden thought materializes in your consciousness like some dread night-specter. The apparition astonishes and dismays you, even as it whispers its sweetly seductive message to your brain: "I am your way out."

You dismiss the foul being from your presence with rough contempt, yet with less roughness than you would have done at more hopeful times, when not caught in this hopeless grinding-to-a-stop of all forward motion in your life. You would like to deny the slightest susceptibility to such an unthinkable solution to your problem, but your suddenly racing heart and the break of illicit light that penetrated your black night of despair and desolation are witnesses against you. You suddenly see yourself with all the weaklings, as you called them, of the race, whose rationale you now understand. But then the you of old asserts itself, new resolutions recharge you with energy and press you to find a way out. You rebuke yourself for slackness of will and weakness of purpose. Your situation must have a solution short of—you can hardly bear to think the word—suicide.

You take up new and harder cudgels. You have summoned a Samurai to contend with the many-limbed and Hydra-headed beast that keeps you in the tight, airless cave of binding circumstance.

What exactly is the problem? It takes as many forms as the varieties of human experience. Your health has broken down, your credit has run totally out, your money is exhausted, your friends refuse you, your children give you no pleasure, your lies, cruelties, thefts, games, connings, idlenesses, stupidities, no longer can be concealed from people who trusted you, cared for you, admired you, loved you. You do not doubt that God himself has turned His face from you, if indeed there is a God, which lately you have begun to doubt. Who are you to stand dutifully at your post like that brave soldier at Pompeii, as the fiery cinders pour down upon you and the boiling lava engulfs you?

You are at an impasse, immured, stymied,

completely so, beyond any extrication by some ingenious leap of thought. Then it occurs to you that suicide, for all its sudden seductiveness and romantic provenance, is not the stroke of a genius but the rather dismal ploy of some benighted churl struggling to get out of his own clothes. You turn away in disillusionment, and suddenly, by some miracle of coincidence, the chimes in your hall clock begin to strike the hour. You listen to each intonation more and more intently, and by the time the noon hour has been fully announced, you are in a position to discover that you have been catapulted for twelve seconds beyond the walls of your previous entombment in thought onto the open plain of real ground under your feet, real sky above you, real trees in your line of sight, real humans peopling the real landscape. Your problem, deadly serious as it was in your thought, close-held as you were by its lethal embrace, real by any test that thought could provide, during those twelve seconds very simply wasn't. Had you inspected your consciousness for the presence of your dread occupants, you would have discovered that, bag and baggage, they had left, and, what is more, left without a trace of their supposed hard tenure. Where did they go? Where does Huckleberry Finn go when you close the book after an evening's mental excursion with him on his truant raft down the Mississippi? Why, he goes nowhere because he was nowhere except in the "somewhere" provided by your imagination.

So you see you weren't stymied after all. For twelve delicious seconds of real time, your predicament didn't exist. Am I trying to tell you that in that interval of time such hard realities as the sorry state of your bank account, your credit, your health just evaporated? Not at all. You were still overdrawn at the bank during the interval, but an overdraft is one kind of reality and an awareness of its implications is another. The overdraft is a bad enough reality in your life without having an awful sense of its implications riding shotgun continuously in your consciousness, and your experience of twelve seconds with the hall clock offers irrefutable evidence that you were suffering unnecessarily, for the simple reason that you were shotgunning yourself. Don't blame the bank or the overdraft for the production in your consciousness of some melodramatic state of being whose presence truly alarms you. When you produce alarming fictions, you should expect to be alarmed. "But," you say, "I have a predicament, it's real, it frightens me, and I want to escape from it. I have this terrifying sense of being utterly boxed in, of being completely defenseless and helpless, of being in a closed room with some rude beast bent on tearing me apart. It makes me panic so that I can think of nothing but escape. I feel, God help me, downright suicidal."

Did you feel it while listening to the clock? Or did you feel, for those twelve seconds while you listened, a delicious escape from that awful room, which was really the room of your constricted, claustrophobic consciousness, the scenario of which, beast and all, you were producing just as surely as if you were in a theater specializing in horror movies. The answer is that during those all too short twelve seconds you didn't have a predicament; all you had were clock chimes ringing in your head. But then, you say, the chimes stopped and you were right back where you had been, grappling hopelessly with the dark beast of your predicament. Well, at least you know how to get twelve seconds of relief from your predicament, which is certainly better than no relief at all—and relief it was, because when you were listening to the clock chiming out its twelve succeeding musical notes you were truly relieved of the activity of producing your state of awareness with all its alarming implications and relieved of the pain, torment, worry and fright which that awareness necessarily spawned in your consciousness, including its tantalizing, unthinkable suicidal impulse. Your problem wasn't solved the way it might have been if you had had a twelve-second telephone call informing you of the sudden generosity of a rich uncle or of the happy reversal of your physician's gloomy prognosis of your health. Instead of its being solved externally, you solved it internally simply by ceasing to produce a melodrama in your consciousness with you as its special victim and audience. You were doing it, and for a blessed interlude you stopped doing it.

Forgetting for a moment the question of the limited usefulness of a twelve-second relief in your life, are you satisfied that the interlude was a relief from your predicament? I mean in the very specific sense that during that interval your consciousness was devoid of an awful preoccupation with your insoluble problems, and if your answer is, "Yes, I must admit that I was blessedly unaware of my anguish while I listened to the clock, and yes, I would have to admit that my unhappy state of mind did not exist during that time," then you must see that, as the saying goes, we had a slice of bologna, no matter how thin it was. We will now take up the question of adding enough slices to make us feel we have something to get our teeth into, for a mere twelve-second interval, welcome as it was, is hardly a basis for unrestrained joy in one's clear and final deliverance from misery.

We have now traded one universe of worries for another, gone from the predicament of being totally stymied in our social affairs to being concerned at the usefulness of twelve seconds of relief, a shift in worries which, even if nothing else were gained, relieves the monotony of a one-predicament consciousness, enabling you to shuttle back and forth from one preoccupation to the other. But this is parenthetical, and lest we be accused of toying with your sensibilities, let us go at once to the matter of showing the full significance of that twelve-second interval as it concerns your happiness and survival.

We have learned that when you come to your senses and make contact with the world outside your thought, your thought simply evaporates, becoming immediately a past reality. It is a further fact that it is in your power in any now of real time to come to your senses, literally to collect your consciousness, withdraw it from thought production, and direct it toward the world of independent extramental reality. Humans possess this power naturally. No doubt an acute awareness of this power is lacking among most people, and without the awareness of the power, the power itself, while still real, is latent, not effectively possessed. Having the power is somehow not enough. The full, and what we may call strategic, use of it requires the exact awareness that we have it. The noon chimes of the clock ring loud and clear down the hall. Our attention is diverted to the sound. This turn of attention has elements of both the automatic and the voluntary. We are pulled by the sound but we also cooperate by an internal act. The voluntary part of that activity is capable of considerable intensification, for you can listen indifferently, oblivious to the cognitive nuances that are involved and uninformed about what is transpiring, particularly about the climatic changes in consciousness produced by the shift from thinking to knowing through the senses, or you can listen at full intelligence with an understanding, as you listen, that you are listening purposely and purposefully. You are engaged in a strategic use of consciousness, in an act wherein the consciousness is made to serve your best interests and not, as is so frequently the case, the other way around.

You need never be stymied. If it happens that by a naïve, poor or feckless use of consciousness, a mental stymying is produced with its toxic fallout to all parts of the body, beginning with the gut, you must see to it that the consciousness better serves you. You must open it up to a plane of awareness on which predicaments and stymyings become manageable, even soluble, problems in your progress toward wholeness and self-fulfillment.

6

How to Cure an Ulcer

"One more such victory," said Pyrrhus, "and I am lost."

ULCERS are the medals of people who have won something, a promotion, a judgment, an emotional battle. Sometimes what is won has really happened and is testified to by the title on the door, money in the bank, a sense of moral triumph or satisfaction. Just as frequently, it is not a real victory but an imaginary one, lived out in consciousness in a way emotionally equivalent to a real event. Both forms of experience know their respective joys and satisfactions, upsets and torments. "Was it all worth it?" asks the actor in the first drama; "Oh, I must find a way to make my dreams come true," groans the second actor, as the gap between the dream and the deed reveals itself.

And though both dramas are lived out in the head, the echo is in the bowels, awash in gastric juices set flowing by the drama. We will leave it to the physiologist to tell us, if he can, why it is that the intestines must bear the dramatic fallout in the form of corrosive acids, which, once their natural work is done on food, turn to the digestion of the organ itself. It is enough for our purposes to note that it is a physiological fact though not a necessary course of events for every individual, or indeed for any individual if his "mind but change its theme," to quote the poet Yeats.[1]

All humans worry, but certain types of ulcer victims do so much of it that normal wear and tear on the stomach does not have a repair cycle, an interlude when it is not fighting off the waves of gastric juices but rebuilding its tissues in a normal routine way. And here the stomach or the duodenum are not making unreasonable demands: The intestines will service the nutritional needs of the whole person cheerfully and well, provided they are not asked to assume the burden of the person's extramural troubles, disputes in which the gut may rightfully claim to have no benefit or interest.

In a sense the gut "knows" when the mind is being used wrongly and suffers accordingly. It cannot be fooled. That is why literature is filled with references to the condition of the digestive tract as a primary witness to the happiness, or lack of it, of the person. Knowing something with your gut is said to be quintessential knowledge, and the expert, for example, who has his head together but not his gut is a wobbly expert indeed. Similarly the gut knows immediately when all is well in the governing part; it relaxes, it does its work serenely and effortlessly; it is happy if you are happy. If the gut cannot be fooled about your happiness, paradoxically your consciousness can be fooled, for frequently the latter takes charge of things and arbitrates matters in ways that are inconsistent with your whole state and permanent best interests. It is you, your real self, who must take charge of your consciousness and require it to send those signals to the intestines which say that all is well. If your stomach is bleeding from ulcers, a condition which foretells the early death of the body should no relief arrive, then you must lay down rules of viable behavior to that consciousness and require it among other things to stop torturing the stomach.

Now it must be asked what it is that the outlaw consciousness does (and a consciousness which causes bleeding in the stomach lives outside the law of orderly personal life) that causes such insult to the digestive tract? This can be answered in two words: It thinks. And if it is argued that that is what the consciousness is supposed to

71

do, the answer is: Not so. For the consciousness is not defined as the manufactory of thought but as the seat of awareness, and since awareness is more than we think or can think it is, clearly thinking is hardly its essential nature or defining principle. Descartes may have said, "I think, therefore I am," but when is the last time that any enlightened man saw that French philosopher as his spiritual father or guru?

> Be relaxed in deep things
> And quiet in little things,
> Like a pond whose shallow water
> Pictures the still bottom as a glass admits light,
> And whose deep water
> Moves not with the ruffling wind.
> Have no thought, but let the answer
> Rise to the surface
> As bubbles rise
> From the lake-bottom springs.
>
> The awakened mind
> Neither thinks nor speculates—
> The awakened mind
> Knows.[2]

The stomach cannot bear uninterrupted thinking of whatever kind, whether it be the kind that is upbeat and, as we sometimes call it, constructive, or that which is thoroughly morbid and oppressive. Too much thought and the stomach begins to groan under the weight, even it would seem before the consciousness rebels, for uninterrupted thinking inevitably becomes involuted and

72

congested, thoughts about thoughts about thoughts which, like diminishing Chinese boxes, end up as an art form of no purpose, amusing but ultimately wearying. We are talking here about prolonged activity of pure thinking, admitting of no sensory input, escape to reverie, insightful discovery, or other states of awareness.

It might be maintained even by experts in psychology that thinking is a natural human activity and the sculptor Rodin's *The Thinker* an unimpeachable monument to man's characteristic activity. On this point I must demur and would repeat that important Biblical admonition on the subject: *Which one of you by taking thought can add to his stature by one cubit?* But, you say, Newton was a thinker and by that activity did he not discover the great laws of terrestrial physics? Rather, he informs us on his cognitive processes, he did not so much think out his solutions as focus his awareness on the questions, whereupon in due course the solutions were suddenly there. Curiously the word "mind" seems to have received its coinage with Descartes. Before that, philosophers spoke more of knowing than of thinking, and the instrument used in the acquisition of knowledge was the intellect. The distinction between intellect and mind is an important one and has a bearing on our topic. One *knows* the life of the tree, the orbital path of the planet; one *thinks* the phyla and genera of biological classification, the angles and intersections of geometry. Trees are out there to be known, circles are thought within consciousness. The former enjoy an independent existence as things, the latter an existence utterly dependent upon the act of thinking. Again, trees can be sensed (seen, touched, etc.); geometrical figures cannot.

Humans think as easily as they know, know as easily as they think. Are both activities then equally natural? The question must be decided not by thought, which predictably would vote for itself, but by some more neutral and disinterested judge. If the gut is allowed to decide the matter, interested as it is, if we may speak that way, in its own prospering, one might hear it say, "Deliver me from those damn thinkers! Their activity is hell on my insides. They're doing something which is unnatural, otherwise I wouldn't be in this torment, ulcerated and bleeding." But then in this matter maybe the gut is prejudiced, a mere material organ which cannot be allowed to interfere with man's progress in thought, treatable by surgery (a product of thought), or by medication (another product of thought) or, not to be too sardonic, obliterated entirely from the scene by worldwide nuclear war and its atomic fallout (yet another product of thought).

What, then, is natural? It is natural for an ulcerated stomach to bleed, for young men drafted in war to die, for human sorrow to be associated with human suffering. It is "natural" for mind to think its thoughts.

The test of naturalness clearly has limited usefulness. There is a man sitting at his desk, a woman preparing supper for her family, each with a bleeding ulcer. They are bleeding not because they have problems but because their consciousness has gotten so deeply into the groove of thinking about them that the alternative mode of awareness, of knowing through their senses the independent world all around them of sky and water, plants and people, is at best an incidental, almost alien, activity. Their stomachs are strangers to the repair cycle that the knowing (as opposed to thinking) states of awareness allow, yet, as deep as are the ruts of habituated thinking, as satisfying as seem the ways of thought (else why would the thinker think?), nothing in nature holds the person to those ways. In the next now, should he so desire, he can be on the path of knowing by willing to listen to what there is to hear, see what there is to see, smell what there is to smell, and when he does, if he monitors the move out of those ruts, he will feel a great burden drop as Atlas might upon shedding his world. Instantly the gut is felicitated, for, magically and wonderfully, the acids attacking it grow weak and ebb back to their glands, though ready to flow again if consciousness enters the ruts of thought again.

How to cure an ulcer? Cure the consciousness

of endlessly minding its troubles, of continuously pacing those mental quarterdecks of fear, worry, anxiety, dread, apprehension, which bring a canker to the gut and soon the whole person down to physical ruin. "But," you say, "I think for a living; thinking gives meaning to my life, captivates me with rare and marvelous excitements. Stop it I will not, I cannot." Stop it you can and sometimes must, for although Rodin's statue commands the critics' praise and the museums' protective attentions, you as thinker will continue to bleed in your living stomach and command attentions medical and terminal if you keep it up.

The shift from minding your worries, from thoughtfully attending to those phantoms of the mind (which come to be intentionally, deny it how you will, in each now of your own choosing) to having the real world in its colors, fragrances, sounds, tastes, textures, the shift from bleeding to prospering, is the act of an instant, a simple process of getting with time the way it really is, for which no tedious arrangements must be made, no demanding conditions met, no artful overtures invented. Do it now and it's done. Do it in the next now and it's done again. Do it thrice in sequence and the doing of it comes to be felt as the ease of birds in flight, the down-coursing of mountain streams, the warming action of the sun.

Thinking has so much good connected with it that its enthusiasts tend to overlook its dark side, the price that thinking exacts, as it were, for the gifts that it confers. These gifts are many. Thinking is the father of science, the instrument for problem-solving, the bearer of speculative excitements and revelations. Thinking ignites the brain with a special fire, imparting a warm feeling of existing, of being alive, of being human. With it humans produce their civilization, raise themselves off the plane of brute nature, evolve and progress. Yet when we say there is a dark side to thinking, we are not so much referring to the indecencies and horrors that thinking men inflict on one another, such as slavery, prostitution, conscription into war, all generated by thought, but to something more sinister.

Thought aspires to capture the world, digest it and assimilate it to itself. It wants to be the totality of what is. We are dealing here with something fundamentally mysterious, even ineffable, certainly paradoxical, because if what we say here about thought is true, it is equally true that there is no thought without the thinking subject; and for thought to take over the subject sounds as preposterous as Huckleberry Finn stealing by night into the study of Mark Twain, tying him up, and carting him off to his Mississippi raft. Therefore, one may properly ask, how can a human's complete creature, which is what thought really is, gain such an independent autonomy as to obliterate the autonomy of its creator? We have already admitted the mysteriousness of this process, and in any case we are limiting ourselves right now to clinical considerations, rather than to the perhaps more fascinating philosophical ones.

Think when you must and reap its many benefits, but know the risks as the gut knows them. Be aware especially that when your thinking has slid seditiously into minding your troubles, into producing those exquisite acts of self-wounding which serve no purpose, it is vital to reenter the unencumbered now of real time. The bleeding will stop, the ulcer will heal, as the harmonies of a consciousness which knows what it is doing, rather than merely thinks what it does, resound through the vital corridors of your whole being. Let us not, as Shakespeare says, burden our remembrances with a heaviness that is gone and, as he might have added, with agonies of a time that no longer is.

7

How to Take Charge of Yourself

For the good that I would I do not, but the evil which I would not, that I do.
St. Paul, ROM. 7:19

YOU know you shouldn't deliberately inhale smoke into your lungs. Nobody from the Surgeon General on down has to tell you that. You know it. In fact it is a bore to have people tell you what you already know. Such advisers insult your intelligence and provoke your anger, implying that you don't clearly perceive, without their help, that smoke doesn't belong in the lungs, or that drinking and driving shouldn't be mixed, that overeating will eventually get to your heart.

So to make them shut up, you invent cockamamy arguments by way of rebuttal, arguments that you don't believe in but which at least gain you some peace from the infernal clatter.

You know it's ridiculous for you (who struggled through high school biology) to pit your prejudiced opinion against the hard objective facts of the nation's head surgeon, but you find yourself doing so anyway, sometimes angrily, often with great passion and sincerity. You won't be pushed around, you say.

Who won't be pushed around? *You* won't.

What you really mean here is that the ignorant, uncaring, willful, self-destroying part of you (with which you frequently and mistakenly identify yourself) won't be pushed around. For clearly no one is pushing around the part of you which knows as true what the Surgeon General is saying on every pack of cigarettes sold in the country. In the first place, if the part of you which knows were in command of you, you wouldn't be smoking, and the Surgeon General's warning would be in other people's pockets, not yours.

And here, finally, on the knowledge of that-part-that-won't-be-pushed-around, you rightfully claim to be an expert. You know that part thoroughly and beyond contradicting. You know its authority and you know its power. You have lived with these for years.

Oh, it's fine for some well-meaning soul to say to you, "Don't smoke; it's bad for you." But you know how often you have said it to yourself, and you know the power with which such a proposal is repelled. You've been down that road at the end of which is defeat after a lot of pain and humiliation. The part of you that wants to smoke just will not listen to the part that knows you shouldn't. It mocks and bullies and dares you to try your high-handed knowledge on it. Reluctantly, the part-that-knows capitulates, doing what it can under the circumstances to minimize the damage, like using filters, but nonetheless caves in.

Caves in? You prefer to call it a "working accommodation," a means of living together, since live together you must. After all, you have work to do, people to support, promises to keep. You can't spend your precious energy fighting bloody battles over lousy cigarettes. Smoking is the price you pay for peace in your whole being. Peace? Well, you feel remorseful and guilty at times about deliberately inhaling smoke, and the habit has cost you some self-respect, but there's a bright side: when you are tormented by hunger for a butt, the craving won't let up on you until you satisfy it with that deep drag and pull to your lungs. So you keep on lighting up cigarettes and inhaling them to get out from under the craving, which distracts you, annoys you, disrupts you ... until you satisfy it. And that's the way it is, you say. For you, and for millions of other people like you: a compromised peace.

81

You have a craving. You weren't born with it, you acquired it. Good or bad, like it or not, you have it. It's a very real part of you. It may not be natural, like the craving for food when hungry, but somehow it has climbed ahead of all the natural cravings—you will go without food, but don't ask you to go without cigarettes.

The point of all this, you say, is that it is a hard, factual description of the way things are for you. The craving to smoke is a reality in your life, a reality that you, not someone pontificating about its dangers, have to live with. And live with it you do on terms dictated by that part of you that is unheeding of any knowledge, alarming or otherwise, that anyone, including you, may have on the subject.

So smoking is not a question of knowledge, of the truth of the madness of smoking from a physical point of view. Pronouncements by a thousand surgeon generals, telling truths a thousand times more substantiated, will not work for you. For one simple reason: the part of you that smokes wants to smoke at all costs, and will brook no interference with its "right" to do so.

The split in you is clear. The evidence revealed by the addiction to cigarettes (or to drinking, overeating, whatever) confirms it beyond challenge. There is a part of you that knows what it should do, and a part that is irresponsible, idle, reckless, uncaring and bullheaded, that does what it feels like doing, no matter what.

Yet to say there is in you a part that knows what is best, that craves the good rather than the grubby, is just to begin to speak about that part. For, being the part-that-knows, it is necessarily many other things as well. Let us see what these are.

If a person is a kingdom, the part-that-knows is the royal part. It can be that the king is badly informed, betrayed by his ministers, under some spell, etc., in which cases he is a disabled king, unfit to rule while in that condition. But if he is truly the king, once those restrictions have been overcome he will demonstrate it in word and deed. He will rule and govern, as befits his role and nature. His subjects will hear his voice, do his bidding, and the whole kingdom will flourish. Underlying it all is the fact that the king knows he is the king and the subjects know it, too.

Knowledge is the sign of the larger reality. Where the knowledge resides, there at least potentially is the power to act, to do. But, as in the case of the inactive king, or the split person, the mere possession of knowledge is not enough. The knowledge must be operational, else the subjects lead ungoverned lives in the kingdom . . . and the part-that-drags fends for itself in the split person. Both in effect govern themselves as, willy-nilly, they must. Who else is there actively to do it?

But neither the ungoverned subjects nor the drag-part of the split person succeed at what they do. What they spawn is anarchy in the political

83

order and moral and physical breakdown in the personal. Lacking knowledge about governing the kingdom or the person, each resembles the blind leading the blind; the ditch soon welcomes them.

If we examine them in their predicament, we soon discover what knowledge it is specifically they both lack. It is this: *They lack the knowledge of what they should do.*

The part-that-drags doesn't know that smoke doesn't belong in the lungs, that it shouldn't smoke. It is only aware of what feels good as an immediate matter. And unquestionably to the addicted smoker smoke feels good in the lungs. And if there is some dim memory in the smoker that at first it didn't feel good at all, in fact made him nauseous, that he had forcibly to overcome the resistance of the lungs to their first encounters with smoke, the part-that-drags has no knowledge of that at all. It responds mechanically to a developed taste, developed by repeated acts of smoke inhalation which violently altered what was natural to it at birth, viz., the craving for unpolluted air.

The absence in it of knowledge of what it should do marks the part-that-drags as a subject, as unfit to govern the whole person or even itself. Not knowing what it should do, even as far as itself is concerned, it immediately goes haywire when it tries. Ironically, the lack of the knowledge of how to govern itself dooms it to try. And to keep on trying without cease. It takes knowledge to acquire knowledge and this is precisely what the part-that-drags lacks. It is only fit to be governed, to serve, to be the physical vehicle of the mind and spirit's purposes. It has and can have no other purpose, as the facts of disorder and breakdown in the split person speedily indicate.

And when the disorder has progressed to the breakdown, as inevitably it will when the part-that-knows abandons its work for too long, the way back is not through warning signals to the part-that-drags. The punch-drunk fighter, beaten to a pulp, may decide he has had enough; the part-that-drags can make no such decision. It doesn't know it is wounded, suffering, dying. It wants one more drink, one more fix, one more orgy. It craves it. It demands it. As breakdown approaches, as the battered and broken body sinks into insensitivity and torpor, even then the demands of the part-that-drags can be heard, somehow more tyrannical and strident than ever. It shows with unmistakable clarity that it doesn't know what is good for it, and never did. The crisis can be perceived and the rescue can only come from the part-that-knows.

Yet, if there is knowledge of the predicament in this part rather than in that, if the rescue operation can be mounted only from the former, it is still the whole person who is split and suffers, body and spirit together. If, in order to understand the problem, distinctions must be made between the part-that-knows and the part-that-drags, there is only one person, one reality, not two. A mystery, no doubt, how this can be, a crucial one for the philosophers, but not one we need dally with here.

The part-that-knows is really not other than the whole person. But for purposes of description now (we promised not to dally over questions of philosophical understanding) we can speak of parts. And it is the part-that-knows, like the king away too long, that must take charge. It is time at long last to begin doing what should have been done. The implications of further delay are frightening. "I should" has been allowed to wait too long upon "I dare not" with hideous consequences. The self-rescue operation must begin at once and be carried through to completion with a vengeance. There is no other way. And this in the face of the complaints, threats, warnings, screams, tears, pleas of the bitterly resentful and resisting part-that-drags. The answer "No!" must be given to every whining request for postponement, every cunning appeal for reconsideration. The No! must be final and definite. To put it another way, it cannot and must not be a lie-to-self. Only the truth can heal the split, restore the autonomy of the person, win back the freedom which has been lost.

What should be done? The person knows. If drinking has brought him down, then he knows what the remedy is: *He should stop.* Completely and forever. Nobody has to tell him. He knows. He has always known, or at least since very early in his slide. And he knew during every moment of the long descent. At every raising of the glass, he knew what he should do: put it down at once. He knew it when just a little high and he knew it when dead drunk. He knew it after his first struggles with alcohol and all the way to the bottom.

Whether it pleased him to know, whether he resented knowing, as when reminded by his preaching friends, is really academic. He knows, unquenchably and really. He is an infallible expert in what he should do. If he didn't choose to implement that knowledge, it is no fault of the knowledge or of his possession of it. His "should mechanism" was *always* working, always instructing him, always "on." Its "beep" was reaching him in every waking circumstance, day and night. It never went away, even when he adopted a policy of studiously ignoring it. Indeed his drinking was often an attempt, a vain one, to get away from his "should mechanism." It gave him no peace, except when he heeded it, as he did occasionally.

And the unquenchable voice of what he should do had allies. The failure to do what one should do brings penalties, penalties which remind even while they do their work of punishing. Physical: a liver which complains of its mistreatment in pain that racks the whole body; a nervous system which will no longer cooperate, shaking the body and torturing the imagination with dread phantoms. Social: a broken family, rejections by relatives and friends, unemployment, the ignominy of ostracism and arrest. Spiritual: self-contempt, loneliness, bitterness, remorse, despair.

It is as though his "should mechanism" said, "I told you so. If you don't do what you should do, you'll be sorry." And he is: sorry in his body, sorry in his spirit. If he doubted the wisdom of the voice that kept telling him what he should do, he can doubt it no longer. The evidence is in and it is overpoweringly persuasive.

Now at last he does what he had never lost the power to do: take charge. A power long in disuse is instantly activated because it kept pace with him every step of the way, ready at any moment to be put in use. Perhaps this realization surprises him. Perhaps he thought otherwise, that he had long ago lost the power, forfeited the right to it by misuse and abuse. This is understandable; but it was a mere superstition, a view that more closely resembled an alibi for not taking charge sooner. It was something that he let himself believe with one part of his brain even while a deeper part knew it was false, knew that he had never lost the power for a single instant in his conscious life.

He finds he is as good as new, that there is a true king in him and that king is intact; he discovers to his delight that he is strong, decisive and knowing.

And if the part-that-drags is churlish and resentful at having its anarchy "disturbed," its below-the-surface reaction is one of instant obedience and cooperation. It is after all acting according to its nature, which is that of a subject. The surface storms are a kind of inertial static which may last indefinitely and be a nuisance but have no power to prevail.

It is not that the part-that-drags knows that it *should* cooperate, should obey. It knows nothing, absolutely nothing of shoulds, as we have said. It responds reflexively to the exercise of power by the part-that-knows; it previously acted only in a power vacuum, in default of what should have been operating all the while. And once the power of the part-that-knows starts to flow, once the government of the whole person is re-established, its full compliance is a foregone conclusion. Before long it is purring with contentment and ease, happy to be doing what nature ordained for it from the beginning.

The split person is healed at that hour.

8

How to Do What You Really Want to Do

Man is the only animal that blushes. Or needs to.
 Mark Twain, PUDD'NHEAD WILSON'S
 NEW CALENDAR

PEOPLE who succeed do what they should do. It's not that such people have a better "should mechanism" than the underachievers—for example, one which gets the message to them better. Heed it they clearly do, but this is no proof that their mechanism works better.

Another name for the "should mechanism" is common sense, and, as at least one major philosopher has pointed out, common sense is the one quality that everyone seems to believe he has as much as anybody else. There are differences in intelligence, wit, judgment, etc., which people among the general populace unarguably admit to, but not common sense.

This can be best understood under the hypothesis that everybody is conscious of getting the "should message." Loud and clear. Many do not heed it, but here is where factors outside of common sense come in.

In the light of these facts I contend that human beings are all created equal in the natural endowment of a "should mechanism," a kind of steady state, same-brand-for-everybody, guaranteed-for-a-lifetime device which is automatic and involuntary. But that is as far as the equality goes.

Yet it is all that is needed to justify calling the country that human beings occupy a "High Democracy," high because the consciousness of what should be done situates all bearers of that consciousness among the demigods, privy, as it were, to the very laws and secrets of reality itself.

Can there be any doubt that the achievers do what they should do? Any quarrel with the argument that the underachievers and failures do not do what they should do?

Or any basis for saying that the failures delight in their failure, that the achievers hate their success?

Clearly none. For the achievers had their success by virtue of doing what they should do. And however they look at that success, by foresight or by hindsight, it was and is what they really wanted. Similarly with the failures. They didn't want to fail, not really. Not unless Aesop was totally wrong about the fox and the grapes he couldn't reach. Oh, one will hear the rationalizations about the glories of failure and the perils of success, but they are not about the failure and the success per se. Success can spoil and failure can uplift... when properly regarded. But this is only to add to the truth about the ongoing value of the "should imperative" in a human life: real success is signed by a becoming modesty and humility, real failure only by permanently giving up.

The achievers are responsive to the "should factor" in their lives. They listen to it. They honor its voice. They somehow perceive that what it proposes is what they really want to do anyway. Or, more accurately, they perceive that they are the *originators* of the "should logic" in their lives. Thus they do not look upon it as some alien presence, some intruder bent upon spoiling things for them with bluenose advice, but someone they recognize as their "better self," with the self the substantive part of the compound. "Why, that's me, really," says the achiever.

And why shouldn't I listen to me, particularly if it's *really* me, and not some pretender to me, some decoy or manikin bearing my face and going through the familiar motions of me? Or some hustling counterfeit trying to use me, exploit me and ultimately hurt me?

But is it likely that a false self is behind all the urgings toward achievement and success, busy night and day telling the person what he or she should do, if as a result of following such obviously good advice, the person succeeds? It seems unlikely that such remarkable effects as the successes of the successful could proceed from a phony self, a fraudulent self, a hostile self—the list can be made very long and topped by that most false and improbable of all selves, namely, the self-who-isn't-there-at-all.

For myself, I am convinced both that it is the real me which is urging me on to realize myself fully, and that what I should do is what I really want to do.

Urging me on to *realize* myself—the word is worth noting. When I realize myself I have made myself real; I have *become* what I should have.

One asks: Can this realization-of-self be accomplished without the urging and the heeding of what I should do? I think not. We perceive how useless it is to instruct an animal about what it should do. We train a dog long and hard, and it responds to our training. But no pure urging on Fido of what he should do, no appeal to the higher nature in him, avails. Is this because there is no truer self urging a brute on to the higher realms of realization in the first place? Who can doubt it? And who can doubt that if the voice that urges each human to transcend the part-in-him-that-drags, to *be*come what he truly is, to do what he *really* wants to do, were to cease, humans would be brutes, i.e., bound to their bodies so tightly as to *be* them?

But humans are not so bound. Every person has a body, but it *is* not he or she. This truth is being confirmed widely today: Dr. Wilder Penfield, the late renowned Canadian neurosurgeon, writes:

> Inasmuch as the brain is a place for newly acquired automatic mechanisms, it is a computer. To be useful, any computer must be programmed and operated by an external agent. Suppose an individual decides to turn his attention to a certain matter. This decision, I suppose, is an act on the part of the mind. . . .
>
> If decisions as to the target of conscious attention are made by the mind, then the mind it is that directs the programming of all the mechanisms of the brain. A man's mind, one might say, is the person. He walks about the world, depending always upon his private computer, which he programs continuously to suit his ever-changing purposes and interests.[1]

Humans are related to their bodies in such a way that they can and should heed the advice to establish a fitting relationship to them—one we have chosen to describe (perhaps wrongly in this antiimperialistic age) as one of king to subject.

95

And to say this is not to suggest for a moment that we are slaves to that voice of the true self in us. Obviously we are free to turn our back on what we should do, as the facts of human history show. Yet if we do less or other than we should, we suffer a very special kind of pain, the pain of remorse, no small matter if we value our peace of mind.

9

How to Keep a Promise

The truth will make you free.
Jesus of Nazareth

A person must not lie to himself—not if he intends to survive. One must be able to count on oneself to do those tasks which one clearly sees, in the brief moments of intuitive understanding, to be absolutes. One must be able to say, "I promise myself to do such and such . . . ," *and to have that promise kept.*

This truth can be seen in the case of the uncontrollable drinker. Granting self-deception its full due, the fact of his helplessness before alcohol is always felt by the drinker well before the attraction is categorized by any human brain, including his own, as "alcoholism."

The self-affirmation of one's powerlessness to limit the amount of one's drinking is said by Alcoholics Anonymous theorists to be the necessary submission to truth which must precede any real steps to sobriety. The "alcoholic" must perceive and implement the simple truth about himself. It is his self-deceiving (his lying to self) that does him in rather than the alcohol, as he struggles to escape by means of alcohol from the self-contempt engendered by breaches of faith with himself, and gets caught in a double bind.[1]

The way out of this crippling double bind is through making a promise-to-self-which-is-not-a-lie that one will *not* lie. One now sets one's face against lying with the deepest and sincerest resolve of which one is capable. A *solemn* compact with oneself is made, based on the clear understanding that one is on the final ground of one's very survival. It is a compact which, upon due performance, guarantees success and suffuses the compact-maker with supreme confidence in its efficacy. Predictably so, because the compact-maker has now occupied a final stronghold, a true ground of being. His task now is a simple one: he must affirm and implement the truth for the best of all reasons, *because it is.*

The self-promise-which-is-not-a-lie is programmed for success. A man realizes that the attraction which alcohol, for example, has for him, is too strong to control by ordinary means. All his best resolves to limit or to stop drinking have proved unavailing. He has broken every promise made, whether to himself or to others. This is because these promises were flawed, promises-made-to-keep-the-peace, egoistic promises and, therefore, not really promises at all. Unrooted in reality, they harbored a lie at the core and were swept away in the first test of strength with the temptation to "have just one." The "alcoholic" needs now to make a *sufficient* promise-to-stop, one that is not a lie. He needs to promise himself *truthfully* that he will drink no more. If and when he does this, he will sever all power that alcohol has over him and will win his freedom from it. There is no other way. It can be said categorically that every "alcoholic" who has gotten free of alcohol for good has made such a true self-promise, while those who have not have not made such a promise.

A truthful self-promise to stop drinking is not just another promise made but soon broken. It is an empowering act which reverses the old master-slave relationship between drinker and drink. Its power derives from the irrefragable law enshrined in the words "The truth will make you free." Once the truth on one's enslavement to alcohol is perceived and admitted, once a truthful self-promise to abstain totally from alcohol for life is made, the

99

interlocking power of such incarnated truths liberates the victim forever. He walks out of the cemetery where all his hopes have been buried into the living land of the free human being.

Truth placed at the center of our lives will not deny us her choicest gift, liberation from tendencies that stultify us. Nothing can be built on a lie but another lie that attempts to certify the first lie as truth by means of yet another lie. Truth, however, is its own warrant and certification. It needs no care and feeding to keep it viable. Unlike the lie, which consumes energy in its management, truth confers energy on the one who courts her.

If the alcoholic, perceiving in his heart his true condition, denies it, his rescue is by that act postponed. If, perceiving and affirming it as true, he then lies to himself about his intention to abstain, his rescue is postponed. Such dreams as he may have of freedom from his bondage will remain but dreams until his affirmation of his condition and his promise to abstain become true. No power to free himself will be available to him as long as he dallies with lies. His vital energy will continue to waste itself on the costly management of his overlay of lies while his real needs go unattended.

But should he at any moment embrace the truth of his condition, and make a self-promise which is true, his rescue is immediately begun and will go on irresistibly to success. Truth will be his instant and perpetual liberator where before lies had been his seemingly unshakable slavemaster.

A lie has nowhere to go; the purpose it served was always one of expediency, never of principle, and any argument otherwise, whether by the liar on the scene or by some latter-day theorist, is always just another lie. A lie demands an apology for itself, and even though the apology be smartly dressed in congratulatory robes, it is no less an apology, an excuse for itself. Lying is always a metaphysically inferior thing to do, even when there is an unarguable physical advantage to doing it. And while truth and reality are no doubt mysterious, it is no mystery why this not only is so but has to be so.

Lying is an attempt to cleave reality. If the lamp *is* on the table and the bird *is* on the limb, then all that truly *is* is implicated in that reality and corroborates it. In this sense, even the flight of a sparrow from one tree to another is registered by the cosmos, shifts the center of the universe, however imperceptibly. To assert that the lamp is *not* on the table, or the bird is *not* on the limb, is an act that flies in the face of reality, attempts to rewrite what is, to palm off a lie on the universe, an act which reality will not allow. For reality is interested in itself, in its own prospering, in ensuring that that which is *is*, and that which is not *is not*. No man can assert that that which is, is not, however great his advantage, without at the same time regretting at his deepest level the act of doing it. No doubt men have fairly jumped at the chance to lie all through human history for reasons of even trivial advantage and celebrated the fact thereafter to all who would listen. But such listeners, including the liar, hold back a little of themselves in the rejoicing; there is a part deep within each of them that recoils, that is chilled by the act. This is one of the many mechanisms of reality defending itself.[2] A house divided against itself cannot stand. There is an impulse in every human heart, however habituated to lying, to speak the truth absolutely, a fact made plain by the guilt that arises spontaneously and ineluctably in the human soul when a lie, for whatever compelling reason, is told.

That which is perceived as better to do is experienced by man as an obligation. Thus does reality protect itself. Man, the real, has a vested interest in reality, is implicated in it, is one of its allies. Consistent with this fact is the deep call in his being to patronize being, to facilitate its operation, to corroborate its activity. The man who does not do what he ought, who does not choose what he perceives as (metaphysically/morally) better, experiences the guilt of that betrayal deeply in his heart, gainsay it how he will. Choosing the better, as he perceives it, he is at metaphysical peace with himself, even as he rails at himself for being a fool, an idealist; choosing the worse, he feels the guilt of moral betrayal.

And when he chooses to lie, even though it be to escape death itself, precisely because a lie is a frontal attack on reality and, as such, the nearest approach that can be made to pure evil, his lie anguishes him. It is an anguish that the liar moves at once to assuage with the comfort of rationalization. "I lied because..." It is no use. There is no adequate apology for a lie. Nothing can really justify it, as the liar knows in his heart. If there is assuagement, it is the assuagement that mere distraction brings. But when the distraction ends, the liar is left with his tortured conscience.

We come now to the matter of what might be called "Proving the Truth," that ongoing, lifelong process in which the self-promiser proves to himself that what he promised originally, say to abstain from alcohol forever, was not a lie but the truth. The drinker has entered into a solemn compact, has made a self-promise of total sincerity and unqualified determination to forgo alcohol forever. He has committed himself by the most sacred and unconditioned vow, made in the presence of whatever gods he honors/fears/loves. He permits himself no thought of betrayal, no hint of equivocation, no uncertainty of intention. It is true that the specter of his old, stumbling self haunts the corridors of his mind and chills his heart. But it does not touch his resolve. He will not be deflected by any amount of knowledge of past failures—*because never before has he put behind him every trace of equivocation, every scintilla of self-deception, every mask, every piece of guile, every lie.* He has sealed off the sorry past from the

103

present and prevented any contamination of the future. This time will be different: he feels it and he knows it.

Now he must *prove* it. What he has promised is this: *To struggle to keep the self-promise from becoming a lie.* And if his promise is *truly* made, the truth inherent in that promise has made him free.

Can the person, for so long habituated to some fatal habit, so long the ready and willing slave of it, get free of it by a single act of self-promising? Yes. A single act of self-promising, really meant, unconditionally given, can liberate him totally. Truth has that power; blessedly so.

But, you ask, how about the person who promises himself sincerely, for example, to give up drinking forever and the next hour or day or year starts drinking again? How has the truth worked for him?

Let me ask this: How has the power saw worked for the lumberjack who left it back in his cabin? The same non-way it worked for the drinker who hasn't used the truth to liberate himself.

Oh, now I get the catch. You are saying that a drinker will get free from his drinking only if he *really* means it.

How is that a catch?

Because obviously a lot of people don't mean what they say, to themselves or to anybody.

That of course is true. But how is it a catch?
How does it invalidate the fact that the truth, really meant, will make you free?

Because it requires a condition to be fulfilled
that a lot of people can't fulfill.

But all I'm saying, and I admit to stealing my
stuff straight from the Gospel, is that if a person
means what he says, speaks the truth, he will get
free.

Otherwise not?

Of course—you can't eat your cake and have
it, too. Reality is not a fool. The person who says
one thing and means another is attempting to fool
reality (which includes himself, other people, nature, the whole of creation, God), and it won't
work. Reality loves itself too much to stand for that
kind of a shuck.

I see what you mean.

I mean simply this: The truth will make you
free. No kidding.

Patanjali, the ancient Hindu sage, left us with
this profound wisdom about the nature of truth and
of truth-telling:

> When a man becomes steadfast in his abstention
> from falsehood, he gets the power of obtaining for
> himself and others the fruits of good deeds,
> without having to perform the good deeds himself.[3]

Patanjali spoke of the perfect freedom of the
"steadfast" truth-teller, one whose words alone

are sufficient proof that he has attained freedom. With him there is not even the faintest hint of a threat against the unity of the real. Accordingly there is no unresponsiveness on the part of reality to the call of his voice: the very winds and the sea obey him (Luke 8:25). But can it be that for those who have (even once) lied, such is the corrupting power of the lie and such the protective recoil of reality against it, that the perfect freedom of the "steadfast" truth-teller is but an Eden, dimly remembered, and pined for only in the deeper precincts of the uncorrupted heart, a small bright light of freedom toward which the cave dwellers of this anguished race of prisoner-men feel impelled to grope?

10

How to Master Time

"It's a long way to Suez."
"It ain't a long way Man, it's just you got a short mind."
              Gary Snyder, EARTH HOUSE HOLD

*F*OR an act of self-promising to work, to liberate the person from his bondage to a weakness or vice, some conditions must be fulfilled, of which the primary and most important is truth. The promise-to-self, as we have said, must not be a lie, which is not a promise at all but a worthless imitation, a counterfeit. What I am talking about is a real promise, not a phony one.

A real promise is one that I intend to keep, unconditionally; meaning not if I can, or if I get the necessary cooperation, but one, simply, that I *will* keep. Forever? Forever is a long time. Is there a way to master time? Yes—by understanding what it really is.

Successful self-promising does not necessarily involve a commitment to forever. But it does necessarily involve a commitment to the now. But, you may well ask, is that long enough? To which the correct answer is: Absolutely yes, for all *real* time is now, the time when absolutely everything occurs. This means that if you stop drinking *now*, you will have stopped, period. There is never a time outside of now in which to do any drinking.

Ah, you may say, that is all well and good theoretically, but look here: if I am on a six-day trek across a waterless desert, I had better carry enough water for the whole trip and not just for one day or for any given now. The future is real too, as I will find out to my sorrow, if I haven't provided for it properly.

The trouble with the waterless desert argument is that as an analogy illustrating the nature of time it limps badly. Desert travelers may run out of water, but no one who is still alive will ever run out of nows. Thus one doesn't have to save nows, like water, for a long life. *Nows are constitutive of life,* the way hydrogen and oxygen are constitutive of water.

The only ingredient a person needs to keep a self-promise-*not*-to-do-something (as opposed to a promise to do something, a promise which may require some temporal ingredient like money or water to carry out) is a supply of nows.

The promise-to-self to stop drinking *now* has no real impediment in the way of its being kept. It needs to be kept only in a now and, as is unarguably true, every human life has an unfailing supply of them as long as life endures. Thus, the description of real time as consisting entirely of nows is not only theoretically true, but true practically, as well.

Yet if humans are always in the time of the real now, being human carries with it the ability to "escape" the real now and enter at will both past time and future time, by using the power of the memory and the imagination, respectively.

The habitual drinker can both remember and imagine. He can, and frequently does, remember how often he tried unsuccessfully to stop drinking. That remembrance, coupled with the thought of the long years ahead of struggling with abstinence, terrifies, discourages and defeats him. He says to himself, "In view of the way I was, I can clearly see how I will be." His fallacy is this: he confuses his real life, past and future, with a vision of it in his mind; he is mistaking the map for the territory.

Visualizing one's life globally has its uses, but it calls for a special caution. Life is really lived in single units of nows, moment after moment. Even the acts of remembering what happened, or of imagining what is to come, take place in real, or now, time. "The Way It Was," or "The Way It Will Be," are states of mental being as contrasted with "The Way Things Are," that is to say right now— which is a state of extra-mental or objective being. Mental states exist only when they are thought; extra-mental states, like the typewriter before me, enjoy an independent existence.

And since future time has only mental existence, one cannot *really* promise anything in it. Humans habitually do, it is true, but at their peril. One can safely promise only to do something now.

It is true that one can rationally say, "I promise to give up drinking forever," but it should be the forever of real nows, not the forever of imaginary time. The distinction I am making here is clearly in line with the urgent advice given by the Alcoholics Anonymous code to drinkers to "live only one day at a time." Living "two days at a time" gets one on the slippery, unreal skids of imaginary time. Thus the distinction I am making is more than a philosophical fine point. It is of the utmost practical value and application. Forever, as I said earlier, is a long time. It is more than that, it is intimidating time, time which can wreck a self-promise by the sheer imaginary "weight" of it. It is phantom time, demon time, time which is no time at all, yet paradoxically has the power to make cowards of us if we try to cope with it. "Sufficient unto the day is the evil thereof," says the Biblical proverb. Sufficient the now for accomplishing all human purposes, too. And totally insufficient any "time" outside of it.

So the second condition for the act of self-promising to work is that it be made about real time. One promises to keep from drinking for a *lifetime* of nows, if that is what is necessary according to one's true perceptions of the case, with the emphasis on the now. When tomorrow or next year becomes now, *at that moment and that moment only* you will forgo alcohol, according to your promise. Thus you will not anticipate any struggles, or imagine any problems. When the time comes, you will hold to your promise just as you hold to it now.

Which brings us to an important fact about time, that it tends to erode experience. A year after a close call with personal disaster, the lucky escapee will be carrying general impressions of his predicament but no longer feel the sharp, painful reality of it. His mind will play tricks on him. He may ask himself was it really all so dangerous, all so serious? Perhaps he exaggerated, perhaps he overreacted.

This is understandable: the keenest memory cannot reproduce in full reality the now-experience of pain, of grief, of remorse.

Not that the experiences will ever be totally effaced. Nobody who has stood on the edge of the precipice and looked into the black and awful void stretching out before him ever completely forgets it. It has marked him forever. Yet, as horrible and searing to the soul as that experience is, time will erode it: it will lose not only its terrifying power but, alas, its very power to alarm and then to motivate.

And as the motivating power of the glimpse of doom is reduced, something must move in to take its place. But what can that be? Surely nothing will motivate the hand never to touch the hot stove again like the actual experience of the pain that accompanies it.

Can it be the strategy of keeping the experience of the pain or grief or remorse alive and real by what might be called "simulation exercises"? By conjuring up the terror again through some kind of carefully controlled but nonetheless scary vicarious experiences? All this short of taking up again actual drink or drugs, of course.

No, such exercises will not work for the simple reason that they are invented, artificial, and known to be so. There is no real moral equivalent to war, certainly not sitting through a three-hour portrayal of "Midway," or "D-Day," however dramatically portrayed. And there is no moral equivalent of the near brush with hell that an alcoholic at the bottom of his dark journey knows. There is no way to fake it, no way to reproduce it "as it really was."

What then can motivate for a lifetime if the experience of hell itself cannot? There is something, and it is the subject of the next chapter.

11

How to Make
It Happen

I shall return.
> *General Douglas MacArthur*

WHEN someone has promised you to do (or not to do) something, he has performed an act which uniquely in human affairs creates a draft on the future. It is an act of moral gravity, obligating the person who made it. "But you promised!" is the adequate and ultimate rebuke to the reneger.

The promiser is held to performance for one reason, a reason which needs no justification beyond itself: A promise was given.

Failure to perform on promises is serious social business. One does not go blithely around

113

society making idle promises; one soon finds out there is a stern social law—I think we may call it a law—governing the making and keeping of promises. In the Old West a man's word was his bond for one very important reason: If he didn't keep it, he was shot.

The social rule or law, as old as human history, is this: Don't make a promise unless you intend to keep it; if you do make it, by God, keep it.

We come then to the idea of promise as the cause of conduct, an idea which turns up everywhere our glance falls on human society, past or present. Let us mention just a few of the well-known instances of this fundamental truth about human dealings.

In religious culture we have the term "the Promised Land." God is said to have promised a special section of the planet's surface to the Jews. And the Jews have held Yahweh to that promise ever since; modern Israel cannot be understood apart from that promise.

Again, for Christians, Christ is the savior who was promised by God after the sin of Adam. In the "fullness of time" that promise was kept through the Incarnation.

In secular affairs perhaps the most famous recent promise made was by Douglas MacArthur upon his departure from the Philippines in World War II. "I shall return," he said. And it must be noted that his eventual return was against the background of that promise, without which it would hardly have had the human force it did.

More modest in scope, no doubt, but still the stuff of legends, was an incident involving the famous home-run hitter Babe Ruth. As the story goes, one day at the peak of his career he arrived at the stadium after a visit to a dying boy in the hospital. The boy had one request: he wanted his hero to hit him a home run. Ruth told the youth that he would do so for him at the game that afternoon. Ruth not only did so, he called the exact pitch that went out of the ballpark for a home run. He had kept his promise to the boy. The crowd, which had been informed of the visit and of the precise prediction, went wild.

Clearly there is an intensity that inheres in a promise that makes it unique. It provides a precise focusing of future time, removing much of the unbearable uncertainty of it, giving it a special value and power.

But our interest in the promise has to do with another matter entirely. It has to do with what I have termed "the Promise as Cause of Conduct." Let us examine this aspect of the promise more closely.

You have made a true promise about real time, explicitly and precisely. Which is to say you made it with every intention to keep it. Let us again say your promise was to stop drinking for good. And such was the quality of your suffering that it has enabled you to keep your promise until now. It has been a full year since you took a drink. Already the horrors of your past enslavement have begun to fade. You are simply beginning to forget how bad, how unbearable it was. Your first days, weeks, months of sobriety were heaven in contrast to those terrible former years. Slowly, as each day passes, that important contrast, motivating you so powerfully, is weakening. You realize it and it worries you. Worse than that, it upsets you and sometimes brings you nearly to a state of panic. How will you keep going, keep sober?

You have made a true promise about real time, have you not? You meant it to be binding on you forever, did you not? You answer "Yes!" to both questions. Well, then, is the promise still binding? Yes. Is it also as real and as valid as the day you made it? Yes. In fact, when you examine your consciousness you find that, while many experiences have faded in sharpness and intensity, one in particular has not, namely, the experience of the promise you made. This is because there was really nothing in it to fade. By that I mean no intensities of suffering, no bodily resonances, no sharpness of feeling. It was not a feeling at all, but an intellectual act, like adding up 2 and 2 and getting 4, instantly recallable at any later date after you learned it, and with exactly the same force of persuasiveness and truth. So long as the laws of arithmetic remain true, so will your discovery that 2 and 2 make 4 commit you. Equally so with your promise: once you make it, you know forever that you did so, know forever that you intended to be bound by it.

No doubt you must remember your promise for it to bind you. But it is not a problem of an experience or feeling that time inevitably weakens, but rather of keeping alive a truth on which time in itself can have no effect. You may forget your keys or wallet but no true promise-to-self, explicitly and precisely made, involving matters as crucial as we are considering, is forgotten through a lapse of memory. The person who forgets such a promise has conspired to do it, arranged it, and if he can fool others by such a plea, he cannot fool himself.

Which brings us to a couple of auxiliary points about the true promise made about real time, that it be explicitly and precisely made.

The self-promise to do anything (I have been writing about drinking only as a significant example) should have the following two processes assisting it: (1) it should be *explicitly* made. I mean by this it should be made to the self at a level of high awareness and understanding. There should be no vagueness or uncertainty about it; and (2) it should be made *precisely*. The self-promiser should define exactly what he is promising so that there is no uncertainty about *what* he has promised, as distinct from *that* he promised to do something.

In any case it is an error to think that the suffering you endured while drinking motivated you causally to stop drinking. At best it prompted you to make a promise. And it was the promise that caused you to stop. Let us be very clear about this. And, appropriately, it has been the promise which has *caused* you to be sober until now. Thus there is no need for panic. You are still fitted out with all you need causally to stay sober... provided you stay in touch with that causality. I refer of course to your self-promise to give up drinking for good.

Thus if you should ever ask yourself why you gave up drinking, why you are giving it up at this moment, there is only one true, appropriate and simple answer: *Because I promised myself to do so.* This is why, this is the cause, and it has nothing whatever to do *causally* with the hell you went through.

Furthermore, the self-promise you made is a reasonable and sufficient cause for action. It is reasonable because your originating promise was an *act* of reason, a considered and rational, as opposed to an impulsive and emotional, use of your best resources to deal with the problem. As we have said, it was your trump card, perceived as such, and held back until the appropriate time. It was a calculated and sober invoking of your highest powers of understanding and judgment, deploying your will to its best advantage. It was a high-powered rescue operation into which you literally threw everything in an attempt to turn time into your servant, to dethrone it from its mastership over you.

And since it was perhaps your most supremely rational act, it continues as such. It is supremely rational for you, now and now and now, to respect that promise, which means simply this: To do what you promised to do *because you promised to do it*. Thus, if it should occur to you, as it no doubt often will, to ask why you should continue, say, to forgo drinking, your internal response should be quick and certain: *Because I promised myself to do so*. You need never fear that your self-promise is not the reason, inducing you to start a search for the "real" one, such as the fact that you suffered so much, that you almost destroyed yourself, ruined your family life, etc. Such are not causes for doing or not doing something but rather occasions which prompted you into the causal action of making a promise, an action so truly causal in fact that it is generative of a whole lifetime's worth of causal actions.

Secondly, the self-promise is sufficient as a cause of action because it is adequate to the requirements of the now (though not, of course, to the requirements of unreal time). A true self-promise is made about real time, i.e., now-time, and if it acts within real time, it will be sufficient to its requirements. The person who promises to stop now, i.e., in now-time forever, need not worry about the causal sufficiency of his promise. His self-promise was to forgo drinking *now*. The sufficiency of such a promise is clear: it is based upon the fact that the now is the only real time there is, that if the self-promiser sticks to his promise, which is a promise obligating him only to now-time, he cannot fail to avoid the first drink.

The sufficiency of the self-promise made about real time presupposes of course that the promiser stay in real time, which is to say that he remain his own contemporary. The sufficiency of the promise as cause is only for *now-time*. Given that sufficiency, it is accurate to call the task of keeping the promise "easy." But the opposite is true for time which is not real, i.e., for imagined or remembered time. There is no promise which is sufficient for "unreal time," as I have called it. This is because the "weight" of such time is infinite, in the sense that it has no confines or measure. This is why the thought of giving up drinking "forever" is so devastating and demoralizing to the compulsive drinker who contemplates it: forever is such a long, long time. To put it more accurately, it is such a long, long *non-time*. One's finite resources are felt to be unequal to such a reach of "time." One feels beaten before one starts, saying intuitively, "No! I cannot do it, so I will not even try."

The perception is an accurate one. Even with the best of promises, one cannot cope with what is unreal. And this is why it is necessary to be clear about what the promise entails about time, namely that *the promise is about now-time and only about now-time.*

The promise as cause of conduct must be the real cause of conduct. When it is, it is the reasonable and sufficient cause for keeping one's promise. It does what it should do: it acts to produce the effect of determining human action. Using the promise the self can safely and securely guide itself to whatever destination it sets for itself. Like the well-supplied desert traveler, it always has enough of what it takes to make the journey successfully, for as long as there is a need to act according to one's self-promise, there will be a now, arriving just on time, in which to carry it out.

12

How to
Trust Yourself

This above all: to thine own self be true . . .
Polonius, HAMLET

A promise is serious business: it cannot be broken with impunity. A promise is a place to stand, a place to say no to any number of previous yeses hurtling you along to ruin; and if it is not kept, the ground of your stand is immediately cut away.

The laws and dynamics of self-trusting are quite simple: You will not distrust yourself until you betray yourself; you will not trust yourself again until you start faithfully keeping the promises you make to yourself.

Let us consider again compulsive overdrinking. You know you should stop it, have often told yourself you would "when the time came," but the time never came—you continued to do what you shouldn't do. This was a game you played, seemingly harmless—how wrong you were!—but in your view all is far from lost. You believe that if it ever becomes necessary, you could stop. Let us say that time has now arrived: unless you stop immediately, irreversible disaster will overtake you. You are at a watershed in your life: you are about to make a promise to yourself to stop drinking for good. You have been playing a dangerous game, a game which you can win provided you use the one trump card remaining to you, namely, trust in yourself. This means that you are about to make a promise to yourself that you will have to keep... or else. Or else what? Or else you will cut out from under you the last ground you have to stand on: belief in yourself. You will have alienated by a betrayal the last and best friend you have, yourself—a far more serious matter than any interpersonal loss.

An oversimplification and melodramatization? Only in the sense that we are not at this point recognizing the possibility of recovering self-trust once it has been lost. For lost it will be (in that immediate time-frame) by a breach of trust in one's own solemn promise-to-self. Not irrecoverably lost, like a finger ring dropped from an oceangoing vessel, but sorely missed and in need of being found again. Thus the loss of self-trust from a single betrayal of self is a *real* loss, one that can *never* be restored to its primal condition. A watch that once stops will never be completely trusted again, unless the cause is discovered and corrected. Let us consider an example, seemingly trivial.

One day you decide that for your health's sake you should do twenty minutes of sit-ups a day. So you promise yourself that tomorrow upon rising you will start the exercises and keep them up for a year. Confidently you put the matter aside until the morning. You rise and your promise occurs to you. You feel sleepy and so you decide not to bother. Instead you spend the time reading the morning paper. Then you are off to work. During the day someone at the office remarks that you have gained some weight. This disturbs you. You resolve to do something about it. Twenty minutes of sitting-up exercises tomorrow morning is what you need? Indeed, that is just what you need. You will promise yourself that tomorrow morning you will start? How can you expect such a promise to be kept by you? You broke that very promise to yourself that very morning! You have cut the ground out from under yourself so that you have no place to stand.

The problem is a real one and relates to our very first point in this chapter: promises are never broken with impunity. There is always a price that must be paid. What is the price that you must now pay for breaking your promise to yourself this morning? Very simply, you have destroyed your own self-credibility on this particular matter. You must wait now to see if you actually will keep your new promise to yourself to commence your exercises when you rise. Yesterday you made the promise and didn't think of it again until you reneged on it. Now you wonder, rightfully, *if* you will keep it. To ensure that you will, you make a special, almost solemn, promise, that you will keep it. You do so because you no longer have much confidence in your ordinary promises, having just broken one.

Now suppose when you get up the next morning, you decide that you will postpone the exercises again. Where will this put you if you try to make a third promise during the day to do sitting-up exercises the next morning? Will an ordinary promise do it? Not likely. Will a special promise? Again, you tried that and failed. What is likely to do it for you? (Let us presume that your heart is in it, that you see the need for it, and that your daytime promises are genuine ones.) A solemn promise? A promise made with an oath, on your mother's grave, before God...? Let us hope. But if that isn't enough to make you keep it the next morning, what have you left? What can you do to ensure that you will do what you want to do? Really nothing. If your solemn promises don't work, you have nowhere to stand. You can make no plans about that particular objective; you are at the mercy of the whim of the moment, the regime of whatever appetite happens to assert itself. And it is not a good position to be in, as you are from time to time acutely aware.

If this example, trivial perhaps in itself, though not in its emotional or spiritual effect upon you, is now extended to the whole scenario of your life, it is clear at once that you are in mortal danger. The person who has lost all trust in his ability to keep his promises to himself is little more than a zombie, a walking dead man. His kingdom is without a king and the anarchy of the subjects of that kingdom is evident everywnere.

A promise, as we said, can never be broken with impunity. The breaking of a promise can lead to failure, to disaster.

Failure—one of the sorriest words in the language. Somehow it is the ultimate indictment. To have to say to yourself, "I failed," is perhaps the cruelest self-accusation only dismally relieved by the excusing words that precede it, "Well, I tried." Surely a consolation. And if you did not at least try? Where is the consolation then? There is nothing to relieve the unhappiness, frequently the misery, that the thought of failure carries with it as its awful child.

Yet failure means little, is even undefinable,

apart from goal-setting. Animals, after all, don't fail. They have no goals, no plans outside what is provided instinctively for them by nature. Humans, however, can be said to fail—but only those humans who set out specifically to do something. Thomas Dewey failed to become President, but presumably not Mickey Mantle, who, instead, tried to be a successful baseball player and succeeded.

The person who promises himself to do sitting-up exercises the next morning, and doesn't, has failed as surely as Thomas Dewey. It is not a public or conspicuous failure, but it is still a failure and it is perceived as such in the consciousness of one man who is thereby diminished. Perhaps he should have made no such promise rather than diminish himself in that way, undercut himself and open himself to a loss of confidence which might lead to something more serious.

It is a dilemma. Promising involves risks and damage if the promise is not kept, but so does the failure to make and keep promises. If you make and keep no promises, you do not grow and develop; if you do, there is the inevitable damage that comes with reneging. What is one to do? The risk of failure must be taken. Growth is a vital, indispensable property of human life, both in the biological and spiritual realm. There can be no standing still for the living human person. Thus promises must be made, to self, to others, and they must also be kept, if growth is to take place and be sustained. This is so for a very simple reason illustrated by the failure to perform those promised morning exercises—if promises are not kept with some consistency, *the power to make them will atrophy. Promises are made because earlier promises were kept.* There is an ineluctable logic to the whole process, a logic that I hope has now become clear.

But again, what of failure? Is there no way back from the breach of the solemn self-promise? Do humans in their promising occupy such a narrow corridor of possibility that there are no second tries, no comebacks from self-betrayals?

Fortunately for man there is no way to fail globally, but only in particular nows. Global failure is an abstraction, a concept associated with fictional time—specifically, remembered time. True, recurring now-failures have their cumulative effect on the person, but even a lifetime of failures does not weigh determinatively on the current now: each now is a free, untrammeled moment. A person fails or succeeds freely in each now. He may be involved in a retrospective evaluation of his career up to that moment, characterizing it a "failure," but this is essentially "fiction writing," a conceptual production having a reality quite distinct from the reality of things in real time, and should be regarded as such. There is no requirement in nature that such fictional states of being have validity, though of course with conventional thinkers they do.

I have already spoken of the way in which fictional states of mind, which are always outside real time, can influence conduct. The person who allows himself to be intimidated by past failures, or panicked by his thoughts about the future, will be hard-pressed to keep or even to make a promise about his conduct. Perhaps he realizes that such a promise would only work now but not later. In this realization of course he is correct: his mistake is in supposing that there is anything *but* now-time, any real time which is not identical with the way it is now.

This means that even the person who has broken a whole lifetime of the most solemn self-promises is really free right now to keep a freshly made one. He actually, really, failed only in a given now, no matter how many of them there were. Since there is no such extra-mental reality as a collective now, no collective now can weigh on him determinatively. To put it another way, his current now comes "without prejudice" from any previous now, or any set of them. He can start again in any now to make and keep his promises.

But, you may ask, what about the fellow who broke his promise to do morning exercises? Didn't he weaken his self-confidence for the second time around, and have to increase the intensity of his promise with each breach? Yes, but this referred to his state of mind, his psychological rather than his real freedom—to the fact that unless he kept his promises, he would sooner or later be too demoralized to make or to keep a given promise. He remains free actually, even though for psychological reasons he may not believe it.

Thus the broken promise is mended for the person by the arrival of a new now, although it takes the keeping of a promise to self to "mend" it psychologically.

A knowledge of both facts combines into a perspective on self-promising that will truly enable you to trust yourself to do what you really want to do.

13

How to Zero In
On Reality

In the landscape of spring there is nothing inferior,
    nothing superior;
Flowering branches grow naturally, some short, some
    long.

ZENRIN POEM

*I*F the past were just a pest like some annoying insect buzzing around your head when you're
trying to enjoy yourself, it would hardly be worth
devoting a chapter to. One quick swat and the an-
noyance would be removed. The trouble is, the
past can be like a pestilence, capable of worrying
you into an early grave. What we need is an immu-
nity system against such a past or some adequate
means of quarantining it so that any power that it
may have to devastate us is kept under careful control.

To say that the past takes its shape and flavor from lived experiences, happy days making for a happy past, bad ones for a bad one, is much too simple a view. Quite the opposite is often the case, since happy days now past can act as such a cruel contrast to one's present as to make the present unbearable; conversely, a bleak and unhappy past can be the principal cause of one's relishing the present.

We have the testimony of the wisest people of the race, the saints, the seers, the mystics, about the bliss inherent in enlightenment, the joys of entry into that state of at-one-ment with reality, where all conflicts and contradictions are resolved and all relativities absorbed into the Absolute. Listen to Meister Eckhart, the great fourteenth-century mystic:

> Neither the One, nor being, nor God, nor rest, nor blessedness, nor satisfaction is to be found where distinctions are. Be therefore that One so that you may find God. And of course, if you are wholly that One, you shall remain so, even where distinctions are. Different things will all be parts of that One to you and will no longer stand in your way.[1]

Yet we also have our own ordinary experience about the advantages of having a present which does not take its cue or coloring from any past, good or bad. For if I am happy now because by contrast my past was miserable, or unhappy now because my past was such a joy, I'm involved in a system of relative perceptions and distinctions which cannot provide me a dependable ground on which to stand in the now. Admittedly we do get caught up in these relativity exercises, and when their contrasts are in our favor, who can forbid their use? For humans will get their happiness howsoever they can.

The problem is that in every shiny apple of favorable comparisons there is a worm that may have been active enough to have ruined the apple's substance. It is the worm of regret that the past, created by a succession of happy presents, cannot be recaptured, is unrecoverably lost—that "you and I are past our dancing days," in Shakespeare's words. Thus, happy memories of the past necessarily come under a cloud, the sweetest ones bitter with the finality of what once happily was. Strip them of that sad feature and happy memories would be all sunlit; alas, this cannot be done. For time as we humans experience it in ordinary consciousness is irreversible, and the moving finger, having writ, moves on, as the Rubaiyat reminds us. Even those who would use the unhappy past, the better to appreciate and improve the present, must deal as best they can with regrets over squandered time.

No, regret is no mood to have moldering in the corners of the present and sending its miasmas into the conciousness. There must be a way this side of enlightenment to experience the absoluteness of the now, of real time, to get with the present in something of its uniqueness, richness and splendor, particularly since the now possesses these qualities in abundance.

Fortunately there is a way which is open to everyone to escape by ordinary means the perils of comparing times, and that is by letting time come through to consciousness the way it really is, without any attempt to influence it subjectively. This is not something which can be accomplished continuously by the untrained; yet just as, for example, in Zen practice even the beginner will have flashes, so you and I can activate our power to experience things like sunsets and symphonies and to know our feelings about them just as they are in themselves without inputs from past time. Consider the way Bashō, the great Japanese poet, experiences nature:

> The great Milky Way
> Spans in a single arch
> The billow-crested sea,
> Falling on Sado below.[2]

Again,

> Cranes hop around
> On the watery beach of Shiogoshi,
> Dabbling their long legs
> In the cool tide of the sea.[3]

And finally:

> In the utter silence
> Of a temple,
> A cicada's voice alone
> Penetrates the rocks.[4]

Bashō explains his approach in the following way: "Go to the pine if you want to learn about the pine, or to the bamboo if you want to learn about the bamboo. And in doing so, you must leave your subjective preoccupation with yourself. Otherwise you impose yourself on the object and do not learn. Your poetry issues of its own accord when you and the object have become one—when you have plunged deep enough into the object to see something like a hidden glimmering there. However well phrased your poetry may be, if your feeling is not natural—if the object and yourself are separate—then your poetry is not true poetry but merely your subjective counterfeit."[5]

Comparisons are not only invidious, they are built on the quicksand of fictional time and therefore can support no reality which is laid upon them. The person whose sole motive for action is keeping up with the Joneses may not only be involved in exhausting rounds of torturing competitions terminated by the awful realization that the Joneses were not worth keeping up with in the first place, but much worse, has neglected his real interests, as Robert Louis Stevenson observed:

> For to do anything because others do it, and not because the thing is good, or kind, or honest in its own right, is to resign all moral control and captaincy upon yourself, and go post-haste to the devil with the greatest number.[6]

Things are good in themselves and true and beautiful besides because they are real in them-

137

selves. One of the great sins against anything's reality is to patronize it, which is to suppose that anything real needs help outside of real time to validate it; and here no doubt language makes its unwitting and unwelcome contribution by furnishing us with ready-to-hand pieces of patronizing patter whose chief justification seems to be mass usage, as though that can ever be a safe guide. Rather the careful proprietor of his life avoids such pitfalls as Stevenson warns against. He does not put down as "old" the worthy gnarled oak tree that has weathered many droughts of summer and storms of winter, comparing it thus idly with younger relatives not yet tested by nature's vicissitudes. It is not Zen to do so, in the sense that no master or wise head would do it, however commonplace it is for the monastery's recent arrivals. Again, to look at another human being with a mind primed to think about the person (his age, race, social class, education, etc.) rather than to know him as he is, which is to say quite independently of any time-related or other comparisons, is to commit the metaphysically deplorable (though socially common) sin of ignorance. And here ignorance is used with its original connotation of ignoring the real in things:

> Distracted from distraction by distraction
> Filled with fancies and empty of meaning
> Tumid apathy with no concentration
> Men and bits of paper, whirled by the cold wind
> That blows before and after time...[7]

The past is necessarily pestiferous. It is a Pandora's Box of contents potentially disturbing to a healthy present, particularly so when the past-reality status of these contents is not perceived. Admitted under any other flag, allowed entry with any other passport than one stamped with their true identities as transients or even as indigents (since reminiscences are entirely supported by present consciousness in their very being), they become not just potentially but actually dangerous. The reminiscing host who is not actively aware of the reality status of his past experiences is in no position to dismiss them when he gets caught up in relativity exercises, as we've called them, ruinous to his gut needs for things in themselves. For he will slide into invidious comparings, encouraged to do so by the clandestinely willed presences from past time, unless he wills to husband his energies for a more satisfactory use of his present, clearly perceiving this as a more choice alternative open to him. In a word, he will follow the path of least resistance, adopting the slack, commonplace mental habits of the herd, unless he has an intact sense of the powers, energies and alternatives available to him in the now that he occupies.

He can either know the realities of the now and experience his feelings about them, or think his comparing and judging thoughts; he cannot do both. It may well suit his purposes to do the latter rather than the former, but there is no true exercise of autonomy in either case unless he is conscious of such autonomy.

But his main purpose, which is happiness, is not and cannot be served by a mind which makes more than a minimal use of experiences from past time or of anticipations in future time. His consciousness must be maximally focused in real time on things and events present to his consciousness. He must *know* reality through the steady use of his sense-faculties rather than merely think about it. He must experience things in themselves in all their appropriateness and splendor, in all their mystery and marvelous sufficiency. He must be in real time, with the now-universe most nearly impinging on him, be open and responsive to all that the world is.

> So much depends
> upon
>
> a red wheel
> barrow
>
> glazed with rain
> water
>
> beside the white
> chickens.[8]

14

How to Forget the Past

The world is weary of the past,
Oh, might it die or rest at last!
                    Percy B. Shelley, "TO A SKYLARK"

*I*T is absurd and unnatural that something so vital as mental health can only be obtained (or regained) by recalling one's past in the ear of a listening analyst.

It is absurd because only a very tiny fraction of mankind can be listened to, given the intimately individual nature of the analysis, and those few need a large income to pay for it.

It is unnatural because recalling the past tends to nullify the effacing and healing power of passing time, particularly when the past is recalled as somehow still having *now*-status. This, then, doubly nullifies the power of time to blunt or to reduce psychic pain. Michael Crichton makes this point well in one of his novels:

> Our brains were the sum total of past experiences long after the experiences themselves were gone. That meant that cause and cure weren't the same thing. The cause of behavior disorders might be in childhood experiences but you couldn't cure the disorder by eliminating the cause, because the cause had disappeared by adulthood. The cure had to come from some other direction. As the Development People said: "A match might start a fire, but once the fire is burning putting out the match won't stop it. The problem is no longer the match. It's the fire."[1]

Freud held that past events, when not being actively recalled by consciousness, are maintained in what he called the "Unconscious." He did not clarify the reality that such past events had, whether in active recall or submerged in the Unconscious, and it is a fair guess it did not occur to him to do so. He simply was not trained to look at his material with a metaphysician's eye.

Because Freud believed that the past was somehow maintained in present time in the Unconscious (an unverifiable reality, by the way), he had no room in his system for ignoring the past, for "letting the dead bury their own dead."

The truth is that the past has a reality recoverable only in memory, which is a willed activity.

And since it is a willed activity, it is erroneous to speak of the productions of memory as in any sense irresistible.

The "irresistibility" of memory events is based on a false and harmful analogy to the true irresistibility of the thing in present time. Things present *to* consciousness, as opposed to purely mental entities present *in* consciousness, cannot be resisted, will not "go away" by being ignored. The ostrich presumably finds this out, and most assuredly do humans. What *is* in the present, while and when it is, whether it be fire or fugue, bird or branch, wind or walnut, enjoys an existence radically different from the subjective states of consciousness.

It may well be that the precisely *willed* character of the act of memory in reviving the past event and giving it the only reality it has is not always clearly perceived. Certainly the complaint of the client to his analyst that he is "haunted" by an event in his past that gives him no rest, argues that the past can be present in some involuntary way.

In such cases what are not perceived and not taken into account, however, are the resources available to all such victims *in any given now, and, therefore, in any sequence of nows,* to enable them precisely to *resist* the incursion of the past into the present. This is the resource furnished by things in the present.

143

Freud did not provide for the crucial distinction between the reality of things or events in the present and the reality of mental states corresponding to past events. Yet it is absolutely central to any real science of mental health. It is a matter of vital importance to the human consciousness that it, at all times, understands that past events have a past-reality status and that they can never exceed this status in recall. And it should be a matter of importance to the analyst involved in counseling human beings.

The past can play a vital role in mental health. The past truly needs to be recalled, for it is the treasurehouse of lived experience, the indispensable and irreplaceable compost heap of discarded *nows*, without whose steady and respectful use no present or future human garden will grow. The man with no memory is doomed eternally to repeat the past, including all his mistakes.

Dredging up the past and rooting about in its rich soil for truffles of understanding and light on the present and future—with all the risks of turning up the unpleasant and perhaps guilt-bearing memories—is a natural and vital human activity. The risks of confrontation with those pieces of darkness, which time has done its best to dull and overgrow with a kind of healing tissue of forgetfulness, can be successfully withstood if no lapse, even momentary, is permitted in a clear sense of the reality-status of the remembered past.

The past, recalled, must be positively and clearly understood for what it is, a consciously willed invitee to the consciousness, existing by the grace of and at the discretion of the host and enjoying never more than a purely mental reality.

The memory of a loved one's agonized death, for example, will be remembered in the class to which it now belongs, a past event. This only requires that suffering which is past should be experienced as past and not kept speciously alive and "real" by unperceived mental activity. Clearly the health of the healthy mind is inseparably bound up with a keen sense of reality as caused by and in relationship to consciousness.

Over and above the problem of a "reality sense" applied to the workings of memory, there is the problem of what might be called the "currents" set up by the act of recollection. This is not a matter of whether the memories are of bright or dark experiences, but of the very dynamism of the recollective power. Any prolonged detached conscious activity, any activity carried out in abstraction from the *now*-order of things and events, tends to be after a certain point self-perpetuating. This is frequently accompanied by a certain vague sense of misgiving or uneasiness over the "distance" that the act of reminiscing has carried

145

the person from real life in the *now*. Still, there is a seductive charm and attractiveness about the activity which encourages continuation of it. The mind has reached an early state of autonomy, elaborating its own fields and currents of reality. This is a critical moment for the person, and the healthy mind hears the clear call of the objective world and terminates the abstractive process at once. In a test of strength with thought, the healthy, thing-oriented consciousness does not fail itself.

Finally, there is the matter of the planned or calculated activation of memory for the sake of mental health. There is, of course, the one done under analysis seeking to find in some sublimated past event or experience the causes of present anxiety. Here past events are regurgitated into the present, confronted, seen for the trivia they really are (hopefully), and the energy that has been tied up in staving off old, now-slain monsters is made available again for real life. Such is the use of the past in the Freudian calculus.

There is another vital approach to the past in the interests of mental health. It is the way of moral and ethical appraisal.

This retrospection is not a whistling search in a cemetery of the buried past; it is a bold and businesslike mental reconstitution and appraisal of past attitudes, motives and responses with a view to current and future correction and gain. It

146

is not a neutralizing or demorbidifying exercise calculated to redeem or purify the past—the realist understands the past *is* past, i.e., forever dead, unreachable and properly left to the mercy of the gods—but a healthy, opportunistic raking of fallen, dead leaves for prizes of moral and psychological insight and enlightenment.

Such a review will be motivated and directed by an understanding of the intimate connection between mental health and a sense of true and steady moral growth. The mentally healthy consciousness is, first of all, self-esteeming, which implies morally distancing a darker and weaker past. This involves a continuing process of shedding the wrong outlook, the short-sighted position, the unsound philosophy. And this can best be achieved by an unflinching reflection on past actions and their consequences.

In such a use of the past, summoned up as a means of illuminating the present and planning the future, of a past understood as the willed, mental re-creation of what is otherwise gone forever, the immediate self-rescue program will be in no danger of losing its true focus on the *now*.

15

How to Have a Decent Future

There will be time, there will be time . . .
  T.S. Eliot, "THE LOVE SONG OF J. ALFRED
  PRUFROCK"

*D*ID you ever read the short story "The Gentleman from San Francisco " by Ivan Bunin? It seems that the gentleman put all his dreams for a "real life" into a distant future when, retired and away from all the work and drudgery of present existence, he would start "really to live."

At last he is retired, fortified with enough income to last through a long, happy, fulfilling retirement, and passenger on a cruise ship that will take him on the first leg of his long-anticipated voyage around the world. One day out he has a heart attack and dies on the ship.

The ship sails on, making its call at all the exotic places on the cruise itinerary. There are dances, parties, excitement, merriment. But the gentleman from San Francisco knows none of these choice things, his refrigerated corpse lies in the ship's hold awaiting the end of the long cruise and the interment back in his home port.

Living for the future alone has its perils. It is not the loss of the future which is tragic. Rather, it is the loss of the present, the *now*, which passes by almost unnoticed under the long gaze to the future or, when noticed, is judged not fit to be compared to the glory which is to come.

To the thoroughgoing "futurist," of course, the future never comes. The *now* serves only one real purpose, a convenience-for-anticipation. Other than that, other than as a kind of lookout post for what tomorrow and tomorrow and tomorrow will bring, the *now* is gone through as some low, inhospitable terrain or swamp with the high and fair ground ahead on the horizon. Unreachably ahead. The present is passed in waited expectancy for what, upon arrival, is never more than another occasion for immediately projecting a new future, its usefulness that of a springboard to anticipated time.

With such an attitude, is it any wonder that present time takes on a quality of insubstantiality and life seems lived as in a dream?

Because future time is always time-as-anticipated in the consciousness, such consciousness should be called "fictional," its vital contents products of the imagination of the host-mind. The futurist would defend himself against this presuming criticism: What is real to him is real, period. Indeed, what else should he call that which supports him in the dreary *now*, motivates him to work and save, comes over as sunlit with promise, is deliciously his own? What can the "lackluster now" offer by way of competing alternative?

The central question that the futurist asks is this: What is the significance of the *now*? It is a question he habitually answers in a way that makes short shrift of the *now*, giving it the "brush-off" that, because of its insubstantiality, it seems to him to deserve.

Living in the future is like life lived entirely in a novel or at the cinema where, once one is caught up in the reality of it, nothing which is not fictional intrudes. In that darkness of the movie house, which serves both to facilitate viewing and to obliterate the thing-world of walls, seats, viewers (oneself included), the world of appearances—*real* appearances, it would be insisted —issues into existence and takes its place on that "truer stage" which is the human imagination. Images (realities) arise which, to the immersed viewer, are indistinguishable from things.

And, they are images most fair that leave all the dragginess of time on the cutting-room floor and put a "starch" in the *now* it otherwise seems to lack.

The future, which never seems to arrive in the real life of the futurist, arrives at the movies. The movies create fictional time, time imagined, futured time. It is time as it ought to be; magic time. It is *now*-time, too, but *now*-time purged of everything that makes the *now* a "stone drag" for the consciousness that has found a better, a more real, time.

The cinema is a market where future time is sold under the label of "The New Improved *Now*." It is the natural habitat of the futurist, the solid ground where the now, captured and encapsulated, must do the imagination's bidding at last, is made to dance to the tune piped by the futurist. It is the place where the future has arrived and served notice on the *now* that it is not to be disturbed with drudgery and the commonplace. It is the rest stop for the breathless pursuers of the what-ought-to-be.

Movies, of course, are "safe" for the futurist, but there are other places that would be deadly for him. The survival time of the full futurist as a motorist on the open road would be close to zero. It is not the road "ahead" (the imagined one) but the current one with its immediate twists and turns with which he must deal. He must not "take his eye off" the real road, not even for an instant.

152

That is to say, he must not attempt to live in the future while driving. If he pines for the "real" road up ahead, with all the better scenery, smoother surface, his pining will soon bring him to grief in a real ditch.

Perhaps it is better to say, therefore, that the futurist is only comparatively "safe" at the movies. Only his consciousness is captured by future time; the rest of his being continues to occupy *now*-time. His conscious involvement with imagined time will not protect his head from a falling ceiling tile.

We all have had the experience of suddenly being "distracted" at the movies, seeing the other viewers watching the screen. It is a disquieting experience, a bit eerie even as, our own illusion snapped for a moment, we peek at others still immersed in the film. The experience can be disorienting (reorienting would be more accurate), and we find it difficult to "get back into" the film. Clearly, to enjoy the movies or theater, we have to be able to block out the real world and enter fully into the "reel world" of images and illusion wherein one loses the real world.

Yet the real world is not totally lost. Even under the full spell of the dramatic action, a part of the mind, functioning however dimly, understands that it is all an image-world of fantasy. Even though we shiver at the villain and weep over the fate of the heroine, we do not rush to the screen to rescue her from the railroad tracks. However deeply involved we get, there is that part of the consciousness that remains detached, that steadily reminds us it is, after all, "only a movie."

When we speak of complicity by the viewer, we mean that movies are really "happening" in the viewer's head. Close the eyes, no pictures; cover the ears, no sound; shut down the consciousness, no awareness. No pictures, no sounds, no awareness, no movies. What is really going on on the screen, as any physicist would point out, are bunches of organized electromagnetic energy which interact with the nervous system to make the movies happen. Of course, this bit of scientific truth, like the truth that the "people" in the film are acting and are not really in love, hurting each other or dying, must be forgotten at the movies if there is to be enjoyment.

But, as already noted, something is and must be remembered *about* the movies. This is that since imagined or fictional time is not real time, no-thing is happening at the movies (or in any imagined time). The *now* of the movies is not where things are really at, but only where thoughts, dissociated from things, are permitted to wander. And in such wandering, properly perceived and kept under control, there can be much entertainment and surely little harm. It is only when thoughts become fully dissociated from the *now* of things and are "invited" to have an autonomy of their own, that the entertainment quickly breaks down and the harm can be immense.

The future does have its uses, however. It has, for example, the power to irradiate the present with its own quality, affecting the present accordingly. Consider: You are a laborer digging coal deep in the bowels of the earth. Your muscles ache, your ears are assaulted by noise, your eyes and nostrils are filled with offending sights and smells. How do you abide it all? The answer is that, while immersed in your work, the thought of the end of your shift, bringing back the whole world you left behind, comforts you, and along with your habit of work, keeps you going. You are especially felicitated by what is to come this Friday night which will bring fun, frolic, camaraderie into your life again and let you savor all the realities your present labor is purchasing for you.

Conversely, the prospect of years ahead in the mine occurs to you as well. You wonder how you will be able to bear it. You vow to escape from it somehow if you can, but the thought of unemployment, of no income and your family's needs sobers you. What other work, work that you know and whose measure you have taken, as hard as it is, pays so well? You brush away the thoughts of leaving and apply yourself to the work at hand. You try to admit to your mind only those aspects of your future which cheer you and enable you to carry on.

Thus the future, although it is just a thought, an expectation, impinges on you, has its effects and uses. And while to the thoroughgoing futurist, the future never seems to arrive, to one immersed solidly in the present it delivers its full cargo of awaited pleasures and dreads, some unforeseen, others seen but misread. And, in the experience of what the future brings, new dreams and fears are fashioned.

16

How to Have a
Real Now

Now is the acceptable time.
                Jesus of Nazareth

*L*ET'S face it, *now* is when you are living, grieving, hurting, worrying, trying to cope, struggling to make ends meet and hold things together, lonely, baffled, upset, misunderstood, drinking, taking drugs, smoking, overeating, bored, angry, passed over, laughed at, rejected, deserted, terrified, aging, suffering, dying. *Now.* This day, this hour, this minute, this second. *Now.* Not tomorrow, or the day after. *Now.* Not yesterday. Not even the yesterday of hours, minutes, or seconds ago. *Now. Now* is where it's at, where you are at, where the whole world is at. Think of it and you will see it's true.

Yesterday and tomorrow do not exist. You can find *now*—it is in front of your eyes, so to speak, in sky and trees, in buildings, and people. But try to find yesterday. Or tomorrow. They are simply nowhere. And this is as much true of a second ago, or a second from now, as a century in the past or into the future.

We are all at this moment in a kind of narrow corridor of reality or time, with nothing, literally nothing, on either side. Perhaps this fact has never occurred to you. Yet, it is true, and its truth is laden with immense significance for you because the *now* is all there is. The elements of interest and need converge in it.

Tomorrow interests you but, notice, *only from your position in the now.* Tomorrow would not be a concern if it promised not to become a *now.* This is what worries the condemned prisoner: that his moment with the executioner is coming.

It is the same with your yesterdays. Since you expect to be visited by memories, you want to be as happy as possible with them. *Happy, that is to say, in the now.*

Thus it is with your future and past time. If you plan or dream, you do so *in a now* and *for what may become a now;* if you reminisce, it is a projection back from what *now* is.

Since the *now* is all there is, it is clear why

you always prefer to cry, or pay, or die *tomorrow*. If only you can keep what is painful or hurtful permanently in your future, it will have no power over you, since you will always only be in a *now*. That is why a mere postponement of something awful, while altogether preferable to no postponement at all, has limited usefulness, and why, without some effective escape into forgetfulness, or sufficient distraction, all horrors scheduled to become a *now* one day must work a real mischief in your present.

It is also clear why *now*-events and *now*-conduct carry with them a special concern: *the past can haunt*. Banquos, covered with blood, and crying out for justice, always threaten to return to the happy *now*-banquet and turn it into a living nightmare.

It is the *now*, then, that interests you, it being where, unexceptionally, your needs occur. You may worry over a need for rescue from tomorrow's burning building, you may grieve over the loss of a loved one, but both are *now*-preoccupations. *Now*-dread. *Now*-grief.

Go through the whole catalogue of woes, past and to come. Where they resonate, where they disturb and terrify, is *in the now*. Surely it is in immediate time that all worries, horrors, pains, whatever, bear down upon you. Problems which have no reality for you *now*, whether they be actual, remembered or anticipated, have no reality at all.

Thus your rescue must come to you in your

now. If you have been burned and are in the iron grip of pain, *now* is the reality and not the future. If news of a tragedy in your family reaches you, the sense of devastation is a *now*-thing, tearing at you *now*. You see *now* the loss you have had, its meaning for the future, its link with the past, and it is *now* that you crave relief and escape from the cruel reality of it. You respond to it *now* with all your resources of doubt and disbelief, anger and unacceptance: it mocks you; its reality overpowers you. Somehow you must accept it. All in the *now*.

The question immediately arises, how long is the *now*? How long does the *now* persist before it slips away into the past? By how much time is the *now* separated from the future? These questions cannot be answered, or even be asked, except in relationship to reality. Language itself points to this relationship as when we say, for example, "It *is* now." Clearly, it is not the *now* which exists, but individual beings which are occurring *now*.

Ordinary experience tends to confirm this impression. The typewriter I am using is always present before me as I sit at my desk. Yet it will become clear upon reflection that the only way the typewriter can "keep up," so to speak, with the *now* in which I use it is if its being keeps succeeding itself. Seeing this important feature of reality is central to the art of self-rescue.

Time may be said to have three "compartments," the past, the present and the future. This does not mean that time *exists* in the past, the present and the future. With respect to the past, it is true to say that all things which are have had some past. The fifty-year-old man, clearly, has had a past of fifty years. But in order to have such a past, he must be living now, since it is also clear both that he is the only one who has had his past and that having something is a present action. The past is a reality in the present of the subject, measuring the amount of succession that the subject has experienced, in the case above, fifty years. Whatever happened has accreted to his being and is stored up as realities in the subject's own reality, in one form or another. In the case of the man, part of his past experience was mental in character, using this in the broad sense. He felt something, learned something, perceived something. These impressions are now stored up in his memory, some recoverable, some not. This is his cognitional past and this is the past that is recovered in memory. He can look at the scar on his hand and deduce from this that he had a past, but when he is remembering how he fell on a piece of glass on the sidewalk and how it felt and looked, he is causing the past *to exist again;* but only in a certain way, by remembering what happened.

The past, then, exists in the present memory, or more simply in the present. It has no existence of its own, for when a being has succeeded itself, it succeeds *with its whole being,* leaving nothing behind the way a beach-walker leaves his footprints in the sand. The whole part of the being is in the *now*, and no part of it is in the past. This is what is meant by saying that it is real, that it is. If it was but is not *now*, it is not at all.

Nothing has a past which is not in a *now*. The succession of *nows* produce the past in the sense that what happened in a *now* continues in the *now* through the power of its succession. This is what can be called "the *nowness* of the past." As noted, when a memory of some past-*now* is stirred, the beings of the past become real, but enjoy the *reality proper to thought, rather than the reality of the thing.*

The future, like the past, also exists only in the present. Instead of existing in the memory, however, it exists in the imagination. There is no future if there is no succession of being, no succession of *nows*. A single lived moment of being, a single *now*, precludes by definition the very possibility of the future. It is precisely the succession of being which creates the future. The future is not a thing, but a creation of thought, of expectation, and this expectation is based upon "thing-experience," the experience of the march of events, the passage of time, the succession of being. This expectation, coupled with a belief that the future is modifiable in the present (or, if there is complete fatalism, summoned up in the imagination the better to bear the unchangeable, the inevitable), causes each person's preoccupation with the future. Yet there is no future except in the imagination.

The *now*, speaking practically, is when things happen. Nothing happens in the past, and nothing happens in the future. Yesterday is gone forever, and tomorrow, if it comes, will not come until tomorrow.

The immediate question that arises is this: What is the *now* in which everything must happen? It certainly seems very brief. It comes in a flash and is gone. The breath I just took is already past, already history. The importance of the *now* is obvious; the importance of both the past-*now* and the future-*now* in the life of a man now becomes clear upon reflection. Side by side, the three temporal realities, with the present as core, situate a man in a wide experience of being and they work to achieve for him a feeling of timelessness within time. This timelessness is one which, clearly, he knows had a beginning and will have an end, but while it lasts the succession of moments, and his succession of being, seem a kind of terrestrial slice of eternity. This despite all the risks and chances and perils of daily living. His whole cognitional life, operating in the *now*, is shot through with the realities of the memory and the imagination in such a way as to flesh out in a threefold time-experience a single, homogeneous and continuous field of wide, deep and full human life. The instant of being which is *now* is enriched continuously by all the reality one has lived and expects to live. In the present one manufactures the future out of the past in a continuing human enterprise of conscious living. Memory and imagination coalesce with present consciousness to form an existential condition which, while within the given *now*, is outside of it at the same time, and even independent of it in a certain way. This state of amplified being and of tri-dimensional *nowness* is one of the things it means to be human.

To say that the future is not real to a man who destroys himself rather than have to live through it is, of course, absurd. Yet, precisely because it is future, it exists only in the imagination. It is clear that men often confuse the "thing-realities" of the present with the "thought-realities" of the future. This is brought out well at the drama or cinema. The question of whether the events "really" happen, whether the people are "real" in the sense that they are "real" cowboys or "real" detectives, is irrelevant to the enjoyment of or involvement in the experience, precisely because one can easily ignore the reality-issue when it serves one's purpose to do so.

For humans, commerce with fictional being is always more bearable because it is under greater control. Since men produce the very reality of thought, they can produce it to their tastes and preferences. The hero can always win in the imagination or projected in books, on the screen, on the stage. Similarly, humans can weep over the death of a Romeo and Juliet and experience the purgation of sorrow without the bitterness of a thing-loss. The danger is that when something really happens, the first impulse is to regard it as fictional, as not having "happened" at all. The death of President John F. Kennedy indicates this tendency very clearly. The typical first reaction to the tragedy was that it didn't "really" happen, but was some monstrous joke. A very bad one, indeed. The meaning, of course, was clear. A great world leader had been shot to death. But the *existence of the event,* as distinct from the meaning, is quite something else again. Thus for many people began the sad work of confirming a thing-event.

The surest way of proving a death is by the presence of the body. This causes a quick coalescence of the thought or meaning with the thing. Even then the pair tend to resist permanent cohesion in the consciousness. There remain, in the early stages of such experience, attempts, increasingly futile, to dissociate thing-existence from thought-existence. But the thing-event is too overpowering, the clutching at the straws of disbelief hopelessly inadequate to hold back the waves of truth which keep breaking on the beach of consciousness with undeniable insistency. Most people who lived through the harrowing event of the Kennedy assassination underwent a process similar to the one just described. Kennedy seemed much too real to die. His power was too vast, his personality and charisma too strong. His death, sudden and unexpected, seemed to have happened only in a dream, in a stage play (particularly, surely, for those millions who "witnessed" the replay on television). It seemed to lack thing-reality on the grounds of logic alone. "How could such a thing have happened?" everyone instantly asked. "Ridiculous! Incredible!" was the quick response of millions of distraught men and women. It was at once put off as a trick, a joke, something laughable. But it was no joke, no mere meaning, no mere being of the mind. The meaning had existential force; it existed as a thing.

And because Kennedy's death had thing-existence, it caused what is often called "existential pain." This is not the pain of the stage, nor the pain of imagination, nor even the pain of the memory. "Existential pain" is the pain that comes from a tear in the fabric of thing-reality that hitherto has been continuous and unbreached. Life is not the same without the missed existent. Existence, in some way, has been threatened, trivialized, made poorer. It is surely true to say that in the minutes, hours and days following the death of Kennedy, the minds of the majority of the world's population were all under the spell of that death, and the world's population was united in a single consciousness-shattering experience.

However, the "now" of the Kennedy death was soon effaced by time's succession. From the distance of some years, it no longer has the pain or the power to wound and consternate. It has, in fact, become a meaning, a being of the mind, a being that, no doubt, great numbers from time to time recall with sadness and regret. Yet, as the saying goes, time heals all wounds, partly, of course, because new events command attention.

We have seen something of the *now's* complexity. Let us return to the simplest truth about it: The *now* is where *you and every event, whether imagined, recollected, or objectively experienced, will intersect.* Every choice, action, thought, ambition, fear, dream, whatever, must be a *now* event to be anything at all. The *now* is where *it* and *you* always are. The *now*, simply, is the working unit of your life.

17

How to Tune In to Things

Om Mani Padme Hum.
> THE GREAT MANTRA OF TIBET

*I*T is a balmy fall evening. The night sky sparkles with myriad stars, the moon still hangs below the brow of the California hills bordering the Pacific Ocean. Reaching the enchanted ear is the sweet mantra of that night, the sound of the cricket. One listens and suddenly experiences a melting away of cares and preoccupation. What matters more than the delicious reality of the insect-rhythm in the night, as old as time, as self-assured as light, as indigenous as the dark? The question suddenly surfaces in the mind, unanswerable.

One leaves the magical ambience with reluctance, promising—whom? the self, the stars, the tiny creatures of the night—to return and listen more ardently, more appreciatingly, more self-forgettingly to those busy musicians of the night.

How to fill with such irreducible reality as cricket-sound the sniffing puppydog mind that has no time for the full sense experience of one real thing? How to feed on that one sound and experience the rich nourishment that it provides? Was it because crickets go their ecstatic way and humans to their rounds of Babel-building that the mantra came into existence? Was it to restore the ancient, dimly remembered peace induced by cricket-sound (and by wind and wave and warbler) that the mantra was invented? Or rather, appeared, for if one listens to the night crickets with a Tibetan ear, one hears "Om Mani Padme Hum," the seed-mantra of that spiritually fertile Land of the Snows.

If one must be precise, cricket-sound is perhaps not a mantra. The mantra is a word formula given in secret by a guru to a spiritual disciple who must keep it secret. The formula is recited, not listened to, as one does to the crickets, and originated as a formula from the Vedas, the basic scriptures of the Hindus and the ultimate authority of their religion.

Humans are not crickets or waves beating

rhythmically on the beach. There is no one purely human sound such as that of crickets. Yet some human sounds are weightier, more resonant, even more sacred than others. Consider these words of a Tibetan scholar and holy man on the sound Om:

> Om is the primordial sound of timeless reality, which vibrates within us from the beginningless past and which reverberates in us, if we have developed our inner sense of hearing by the perfect pacification of our mind. It is the transcendent sound of the inborn law of all things, the eternal rhythm of all that moves, a rhythm in which law becomes the expression of perfect freedom.[1]

If we turn to Islamic culture, we find a similar rigorous narrowing down of all available sounds to one:

> Allah is the word used to denote the final objectivity, uniqueness, something which has no relationship with numbering, anything in time, anything which propagates in a sense familiar to man.[2]

Again, of a more ancient religious culture:

> For the Hebrews the name of Yahweh, as its word, was a kind of entity detachable from the divine person, a greatness existing in itself, apart from the person.[3]

Among Christians, St. Paul expresses the uniqueness of one particular sound:

> God hath given him a name which is above all names, that in the name of Jesus every knee

should bow, of those that are in heaven, on earth, and under the earth.[4]

Man, unlike the animals, invents language, developing it into a rich and subtle instrument of social communication, and then, chafing at the limitations of that instrument, finds through the mantra a deeper experience of reality.

The word "mantra" is Sanskrit, and mantra-recitation is a practice most strongly developed in India or cultures influenced by it. Yet, it is practiced, whether formally or not, wherever men have come to realize that some units of a language—usually but not always connected with religion—are "charged," that is, resonant with a mysterious charism or energy that recitation releases.[5]

> Needless to add, the practice of making japam [repetition of the mantra] is not confined to the Hindu religion. The Catholics teach it also. "Hail Mary" is a mantram. A form of mantram is also recognized by the Greek Orthodox Church.[6]

The author might have gone further to include such practices by Buddhist, Islamic and Jewish believers and then taken notice of mantric practices outside the religious sphere in commerce, military life, sports and social life in general. Words have power, as advertisers are well aware, and much money and energy are expended searching for and repeating endlessly into the consumer's ear the ones that magically unlock the pocketbook.

The fully developed self-rescue art takes due notice of the phenomenon known as the mantra. It aims at duplicating as nearly as possible the quieting effect upon the consciousness of listening to crickets repeating their sounds in the night.

.... People who have never tried the practice of repeating the name of God are apt to scoff at it: it seems to them so empty, so mechanical. "Just repeating the same word over and over!" they exclaim scornfully. "What possible good can that do?"

The truth is that we are all inclined to flatter ourselves—that we spend our time thinking logical, consecutive thoughts. In fact, most of us do no such thing... More usually, we are in a state of reverie—a mental fog of disconnected sense-impressions, irrelevant memories, nonsensical scraps of sentences from books and newspapers, little darting fears and resentments, physical sensations of discomfort, excitement or ease... Because we do nothing to control this reverie, it is largely conditioned by external circumstances.... The sun comes out; our mood brightens. Insects begin to buzz around us, and we turn irritable and nervous. Often, it is as simple as that.

But now, if we introduce into this reverie the repetition of the name of God, we shall find that we can control our moods, despite the interference of the outside world. We are always, anyhow, repeating words in our minds—the name of a friend or an enemy, the name of an anxiety, the name of a desired object—and each of these words is surrounded by its own mental climate. Try saying "war," or "cancer," or "money," ten thousand times, and you will find that your whole mood has been changed and colored by the associations connected with that word. Similarly, the name of God will change the climate of your mind. It cannot do otherwise.[7]

Swami Prabhavananda points out an important fact, that when a mantra occupies the consciousness, *no other mental construction is able to inhabit it.* The mantra *intrudes,* but it equally and simultaneously *excludes.* And because of this, its use can be a most effective self-rescue technique, a fitting complement to the basic self-rescue technique of excluding thought by attending to the sensible experiencing of a thing.

18

How to Be Cheerful

Imagine a society of saints, a perfect cloister of exemplary individuals. Crimes, properly so-called, will be there unknown; but faults which appear venial to the layman will create there the same scandal that the ordinary offense does in ordinary consciousness. If, then, this society has the power to judge and punish, it will define these acts as criminal and will treat them as such. For the same reason, the perfect and upright man judges his smallest failings with a severity that the majority reserve for acts more truly in the nature of an offense.
Emil Durkheim

THE person who feels sorry for himself because of his "poverty" is involved in an act of comparing of which he may or may not be aware. Considering that he is wealthy in comparison to a Calcutta street beggar, it is clear that he has been looking (actually or in his mind's eye) at the material possessions of those more prosperous than himself, who, themselves, might feel poor if they were looking at an Indian rajah. The rajah, in turn, surely has his moments of feeling poor relative to nature's richness. The person in question, at one and the same time, both is and is not poor, as is every other human being on earth.

But surely the Calcutta beggar, with literally nowhere to lay his head at night but the curbstone, possessing only the rags on his bony back and the scraps of food gathered from the garbage dump, is an exception to this relativistic system. That is to say, he is *absolutely* poor. But, wait, tonight there gleams in his dark hand a silver rupee found earlier in the dust. *Yesterday* he was a poor man without means, now in his mind he is a rajah!

"Poverty" is a state of mind from which anyone of any social strata may suffer, depending upon where he lets his glance fall. "The child of the samurai warrior may have an empty belly, but he is never hungry," goes the ancient Japanese proverb. The father, unable to purchase the medicines needed to heal his sick child, thinks of the stuffed shelf of the pharmacist or the jeweled fingers of the society matron, and weeps at his poverty (and most certainly the injustice of it all). He does not think of the long ages when all men lived in caves and dropped like flies from pestilences about which they could do nothing. Relative to that vast population, he is wealthy. As a mere charity patient at the clinic, he commands for his child a wealth the pharaohs lacked. He has but to cast his mind's eye in another direction, away from the prince and banker and toward the poorer than he, whose numbers throughout human history are legion, to improve his feeling of poverty.

Moreover, he is free to relieve himself in this way, assuming other relief is closed to him. He is free to change the climate of his mind by changing the relativity of his perception. The masochist who marches by the mansions of the rich, whether on foot or in his mind, coveting that which he lacks, is the fabricator of his own torture.

"Bitter experiences don't necessarily make bitter people," G. K. Chesterton once observed. This is to say that there are no bitter experiences that are not fashioned by the mind making invidious comparisons to no gain.

E. E. Cummings, the poet, advises casting one's glance deliberately toward those circumstances which favor, indeed create, a happy and contented interior state:

> .... never be guilty of self-pity; if you once had a little but now have less, forget the earlier time gladly; & when you have least, remember gladly the time when you had most....[1]

The old, gazing upon the blithe skipping of the young, and reflecting on their own lost youth, grow sad. What they must realize, if their older years are not to be overshadowed by idle reminiscences, is that the quality of life at any age is a matter of comparative perceptions which, in turn, produce their allied feelings. That is to say, the old man or the poor man is "old" or "poor" only in a relativity system of his own making.

It is not merely temperament or disposition but also social influences that work on the individual's choosing. Just as there is a social fashion in hats and umbrellas, there is a social fashion dictating where people of a given time and culture let their glances fall. At present, an ever-increasing number of people are using their minds according to unabashed Marxist materialist dogma, as any study of the world's ideological map will show. Which is simply to say that they are making the invidious comparisons that provide the "unmistakable evidence" that economic exploitation is the order of the day in capitalistic societies.

What few understand is that if there is a natural "law" called "the Relativity of Perceptions" to which all men are subject in their qualitative judgments about their experience, there is no law which governs the particular relativistic system that men choose. While the glancing of men is natural, *where* that glance is directed is, for most men, a matter of fashion or of stage direction. In our times, more and more humans find themselves under the stage direction of Marx. Large numbers in the Hindu, Islamic and Buddhist traditions do not (yet?) walk that stage. In Calcutta the street beggar's torpor is not so much the lethargy of hopelessness as the resignation of the believer in karmic law. If there is relative social calm in Cairo, Dacca and Damascus, it is because the relativity system taught by the Prophet is still in force. Of Him who said "suffer them both [the just and the unjust] to grow until the harvest" (Matt. 13:30), what can be said except that fewer and fewer in the West are taking their perceptional cues from His gospel?

The truth is that wealth's only rational purpose is to purchase contentment. Why else do men strive mightily after it? And contentment is a state of mind that is inseparable from the "wealth-producing comparison."

In any act of qualitative comparison the perceiver may easily note for himself that "having less," in E. E. Cummings' phrase, has no meaning except in relationship to a previous condition of "having more." The condition of having more usually needs a time fix. All those who jumped out of windows on that sad "Black Friday" of the 1929 Wall Street Crash did so because their new impoverishment was unbearable compared to a previous prosperity. Among the jumpers were a sampling of every previous economic class from the very *nouveau riche* to the "old" monied. Each person wiped out by the bursting of the great speculative bubble who turned to suicide, had, no doubt, a very personal, individualized reaction to that great event in his life, but at least one generality may be drawn about them all: each failed to invent a relativity system appropriate to a will to live. Many others, indeed most, of that day's stricken of course did: laughing toasts were made to some such lifesaving slogans as "easy come, easy go" by all classes of the previously monied, old and new, the invested and the speculated. It was a saving sense of humor at the conversational level but it was also the act of favorable comparing on the deeper levels that worked to smother the impulses toward "abandoning it all."

The old-monied bankrupt came naked into the world and, if required to go out naked, he can make comparisons with that earlier state and escape the miseries of deprivation that would accompany later comparisons. The new-monied bankrupt need perhaps only go back to a few months or years before Dame Fortune briefly smiled for consolation. It is a free choice and one which each will not fail to make if morale for living is to be sustained.

The freedom to make the favorable comparison remains even when all other options are seemingly closed down, and it is this freedom which is surely the defining one when the matter of a man's real freedom is being argued.

Every man, whether he be Calcutta street beggar or prince, who has the capacity to suffer the mental torments of loss can rouse himself from the miseries into which his invidious comparings have plunged him, to comparings which persuade to a happier frame of mind. If he insists on making comparisons that cause him misery, he alone is then responsible for the misery. The man who chops off his finger in anger can hardly blame the cleaver that was the instrument of the loss.

It is in the light of such truths about the comparing faculty that Shakespeare's famous line in Hamlet, "There is nothing either good or bad, but thinking makes it so, " must be understood. What that great student of the human heart meant was not some trivial notion that thinking, a conceptual act, is the creator of the good or evil in the world, but rather that how a human feels about his lot is often the result of comparing it with a remembered or imagined time. Prince Hamlet, brooding on a happier life when his father was still king of Denmark, pondered taking "arms against a sea of troubles," by means of suicide. The "thinking" to which the Bard referred was *comparative* thinking.

Favorable comparing is not compatible with choices regulated by proximities in time. That is to say, the recent should never be the criterion of comparison-choices merely because it is recent. No doubt the event that happened yesterday is fresher in the consciousness than last year's event, but its use as material for comparison must not be dictated by mere freshness of impression. *All* past events have a reality-status utterly dependent on memory. They once were; they now are not, except as they are remembered. They are "beings of the mind," to use a precise philosophical definition. Accordingly, *all* past events are equidistant from the present moment, just as in mathematics all numbers divided by zero give infinity; once past, the deeds of Alexander the Great are as near to the present moment as the morning's cup of coffee. Yesterday's event is no more valid as a standard of comparison for a *now* event than one a century ago. The man who is depressed because he was rich last year and this year is poor may, with equal validity, find a time in his past conducive to favorable comparing. That is to say, favorable to a cheerful, happy climate of mind. It is, of course, no mystery how the perennially cheerful souls that make up a solid minority of the population maintain their cheerful state through the vagaries that are part of every human life. It is their practice (whether conscious or not) of making favorable comparisons.

What is true of the use of the past is also true of the use of imagined events of the future. What will be can never be known absolutely by the human mind.

Given the true openness of future events, the person who values the health and equilibrium of his mind and spirit imagines those events which are favorable to it. Such a person is sometimes called an "optimist." But a real optimism of spirit is something more than a mindless expectation of the improvement in one's affairs or condition of life. As we saw in Chapter Thirteen, it is the steady practice of discovering and relating to things as they are in themselves, in other words, the wise use of time. It involves a strong faith in the love and care of the universe for itself, in its fundamentally benign character, in a conviction that all finally will be well.

19

How to Be Brave

All which thy child's mistake
Fancies as lost, I have stored for Thee at home.
                    Francis Thompson, "THE HOUND OF HEAVEN"

*T*HE torturer who tries to prolong the agony of the victim soon finds to his dismay that the latter is not, as he had thought, defenseless before him. Let the level of pain grow great and the man on the rack is wafted swiftly beyond reach of his persecutor. Why such a threshold of suffering, a cutoff point beyond which the torturer is barred? Ask the atheist whose reading of the fact of suffering in the world by living creatures is argument sufficient that there can be no God. God, the familiar argument goes, cannot coexist with the slaughter of the innocents, the unrelieved misery of the insane asylum and leprosarium, the hell of every battlefield from Thermopylae to Dien Bien Phu.

The atheist, looking at the productions of his mind, finds no limit to the spectacle of suffering. But, when it is his time for real pain—rather than its melodramatic representation in his mind—he, too, will experience what must be called the "Benignity of God."

One might ask, Why must the victim suffer at all? Surely a truly benign God would spare his creatures all suffering, even as a mother would spare her child all pain if she could.

The logic of *some* pain for her child is something a wise mother understands. Thus the spanking is an important tool in the repertory of the provident mother: pain teaches. Pain also warns of dysfunction and illness. The mother who imposes limited pain on her child, reconciled to its necessity and usefulness, still fulfills the definition of a kind mother.

Living beings from time to time suffer. But such suffering always has limits. Nature makes its point with pain and is done with it. There is no pain for pain's sake, no suffering which does not serve the finite economy of the sufferer, at least not in nature; man's inhumanity to man, admittedly, is another matter, yet still finite. Pain is a signal of the need for repair and, when repair is out of the question, the body having been devastated, there is no pain at all. The man who loses his arm accidentally either blacks out at once or, as is frequently the case, experiences no immediate pain, such is the self-anesthetizing power of the body. The organism wounded by accident or disease beyond restoring capability goes into a coma and dies, putting the victim irreversibly out of harm's way. Death here is the purest benignity.

But suffering is not all physical. What must be said of those peculiarly human sufferings of loneliness, loss, guilt, remorse, those "daggers of the mind," of which Shakespeare wrote? Consider Lady Macbeth:

> DOCTOR: Not so sick, my Lord
>   As she is troubled with thick-coming fancies,
>   That keep her from her rest.
> MACBETH: Cure her of that:
>   Canst thou not minister to a mind diseased,
>   Pluck from the memory a rooted sorrow,
>   Raze out the written troubles of the brain,
>   And with some sweet oblivious antidote,
>   Cleanse the stuff'd bosom of that perilous
>   stuff
>   Which weighs upon the heart?[1]

Mental sufferings, frequently the worst sufferings of all, have their reliefs, such as tranquilizers and shock therapy, pastoral caring and psychoanalysis, and radical surgical procedures such as lobotomy. There is the escape to the temporary relief of drunkenness and drug highs, to fantasy and to the more permanently chosen states of madness. Finally, for the sufferer who seeks the final solution, there is suicide, a way which does violence to the strongest natural instinct, self-preservation, and which is under heavy moral and legal proscription, but provides for an end to suffering.

But what of death, that dread inescapable reality hanging over all of life and mocking its hopes? There is no question that it is naturally repugnant to the human mind, baffled and intimidated by its mystery. The direct look at it is avoided through the euphemism, the devices of the undertaker.[2] The poet Yeats has this advice for those who inquire about dying:

> Cast a cold eye
> On life, on death.
> Horseman, pass by.

Is this the "cold eye" of indifference or of bewilderment, one wonders?

Death does not successfully deflect every glance in its direction, however. Certain enterprising clinical investigations are beginning to penetrate its mystery. Consider the discoveries of physician-thanatologist, Elizabeth Kubler-Ross, about death. Although she used to regard it as a natural termination to individual existence, she now says she is "certain that it is not." She adds that only the physical body dies, but psychic life goes on. "None of the patients who have had a death experience—and returned—are ever afraid to die."[3]

188

Death is feared as an unknown, but some few privileged humans who have had a death experience report that death is a doorway to peace, wholeness and happiness. They testify to a world beyond that is inexpressibly beautiful and undeniably real. One wonders upon hearing this whether the instinctive animal fear of death is not nature's counterweight against the pull of that other realm on the living.

These signs and arguments of the benignity of the universe do not so much require faith as observation of nature's fundamental processes. Living things seldom are very long at their suffering and dying, and never without some natural dulling and relief: the universe does not allow it. The piteous cry of the wounded deer, the plea for relief of the stricken man does not go unheeded or unheard through some long reach of measureless time. No, there is a close and watchful monitoring of even the lowliest creature's suffering, of which William Blake warns tormentors to be aware:

> A dog starved at his master's gate
> Predicts the ruin of the state.[4]

There are evidences in the regular workings of the universe which prompt a view, expressed beautifully by Alan Watts, that "a man may dare to think that he is not a stranger in the universe, nor a solitary and tragic flash of awareness in endless and overwhelming darkness."[5]

The mystics, whether a St. Teresa or a

Milarepa, a Shankara or an Ibn El-Arabi, a Jacob Boehme or a Dogen, all came to understand that the universe is benign. The earth-touching mudra of the Buddha ("Fear not"), the unbounded compassion of the dying Christ ("Forgive them"), the infinite responsiveness of the Father to the needs of His children ("Ask and you shall receive") make full and marvelous sense to those humans enlightened by the direct, ecstatic vision of God's own life. They see what the poet so touchingly expresses:

> The world is charged with the grandeur
>   of God....
> There lives the dearest freshness deep
>   down things.[6]

They see that the "child's mistake [which] fancies all as lost" is but God's Joke, a Divine Comedy, which is sometimes scary but is to have an unspeakably happy ending for the players. Chesterton says it perfectly:

> Chattering finch and water-fly
> Are not merrier than I;
> Here among the flowers I lie
> Laughing everlastingly.
> No: I may not tell the best:
> Surely, friends, I might have guessed
> Death was but the good King's jest,
>   It was hid so carefully.[7]

190

20

How to Find Yourself

Imagine a child sleeping next to its parents and dreaming it is being beaten or is painfully sick. The parents cannot help the child no matter how much it suffers, for no one can enter the dreaming mind of another. If the child could awaken itself, it could be freed of the suffering automatically.
Bassui's Sermon, quoted by Philip Kapleau,
THE THREE PILLARS OF ZEN

A man stands poised on the railing of the Golden Gate Bridge. He is about to kill himself with a leap into the blue-black waters below. Don't hurry over the last sentence, because it contains the key to finding the self. *He* is about to kill *himself.* If the sentence means anything at all, it means that there is a "he" who is going to kill and a "he" who is going to be killed. But, one asks, how can this be? There is, after all, only one person on the bridge rail, not two.

Don't be too easily deceived by appearances,

191

or dismiss too readily the possibility, suggested by the sentence in question, that there are two *he's* involved in the suicide act. It may well be that the suicide is making an assumption of which he is soon to be disabused, that he is putting an end to himself totally. To do so he would have to be sure to execute the executioner, too—assuming there is one separate from the being he is determined to kill.

One wonders what questions he asked himself, long before he left his house, got into his car, and drove to the bridge? And did he ask himself the appropriate questions, the answers to which might have persuaded him to go on living—questions like, Is it the *real me* who is urging a jump off the bridge rather than some chance intruder? Is this advice prudent and wise, corresponding with my best interests? Is it possible that whoever or whatever is giving such suicidal instructions has nothing to lose from acting on them?

An affirmative answer by the jumper to the first two questions might be expected. But what of the third question? From its answer he might have perceived that within him there is a very intelligent being, more real than his conventional (ego) self, sitting, as it were, above the battle and letting the ego-self play boss—however foolishly—having nothing to lose by so doing. He might also have realized there is no way at all, therefore, that he can kill himself totally, for his inner self is immune to injury.

In the book *How to Know God*, which is a commentary on the aphorisms of the Hindu saint Patanjali, is the following statement:

> The "seed of evil"is ignorance. Because of ignorance, man forgets that he is the Atman and creates for himself the illusion of a private, separate ego-personality. This ego-personality is intent upon satisfying its desires, and acquiring possessions and powers over external nature.[1]

And again:

> Therefore a man must cease to identify himself with the mind, in order to win liberation. When he knows beyond doubt that he is the Atman, and not the mind, he is made free from his karma.[2]

These remarks, prompted by ancient Oriental teachings, apply remarkably to the suicidal act of a Western man in the last quarter of the twentieth century. They illuminate the act for us better than the familiar opinions of the behavioral scientists on suicide. Or the judgments that theologians and moralists would have about the act. "When he knows . . . he is . . . not the mind . . . !" This is precisely what the suicide did not know. In his ignorance, the suicide thought he was his own self-conception, e.g., a fool, a weakling, a phony, a parasite, a murderer (the list is as long as the suicide list), and, dismayed by the belief, found the courage to destroy that supposed reality. In fact, he is none of these beings, never was and never will be. What he killed were his own self-productions, entities he could have easily done away with by simply ceasing to think them, a power that was his even as he stood poised on the bridge rail.

"Therefore a man must cease to identify himself with the mind, in order to win liberation." The suicide is not only tied to a fatal, self-produced estimation of himself, but also is tied closely to a self-produced decision to destroy himself, a decision which he doggedly persists in producing as a dominating theme in his consciousness.

There is an understandable but unfortunate habit in humans of succumbing to what psychologists call the omnipotence of thought. A person takes a peek through the curtains of consciousness at the little stage where a couple of his thoughts are performing and sees it as the world scenario. The error of letting one's thought, even though it be about the whole world, swallow the world without a further trace is widespread. The man bent on suicide has declared war against his predicament; he intends to bear it no longer, to dash it to pieces on the rocks below the cliff where he stands poised. Presumably he has no quarrel with his heart or hand, which have always served him well, but which are about to be done violence to. If, standing there about to jump, he could get his consciousness where his body is and where the rest of the world is, he wouldn't be bent so single-mindedly on jumping. He is pitting the impulse of the preempting part against the abiding wisdom of the enduring whole. If he is to survive, change his mind and walk away, he has to get immediately where he really is, rather than where he thinks, in his error, that he and the whole world are.

We get to where we are by awakening to who we are, something that no amount of thinking can accomplish for us. Indeed, thinking is the very stuff of our sleep, captured as we are in the arms of categorized being, assimilated as we are to those bewitching mental states of our own making, to dreams so powerful that they pass for the real world itself. It is an irony for most humans that they should feel most awake, exhilarated by the excitements of thought, at that very moment when they are slumbering most deeply. And to try to tell the sleeper who he really is is to risk his belligerence, for the sleeper enjoys his sleep, will not easily be awakened, and is content to dream on in ignorance of his true estate.

Our would-be suicide needs to perceive the doctrinal heart of all true religion, *that all being is one.* This is expressed by Hinduism in the following formula: *"An invisible and subtle essence is the Spirit of the whole universe. That is Reality. That is Truth. Thou art That (tat tvam asi)."*[3]

In Islam, by: *"Therefore, 'There is no deity but ALLAH' is the Many's declaration of Unity: that of the Few is 'There is no he but He.' "*[4] In Christianity, by the words of Christ: *"That they all may be one, as thou, Father, in me, and I in thee; that they also may be one in us."*[5]

The perception that all being is one would do many things for its host. It would enhance his self-esteem through the realization that he is not some foreign substance in the universe better off eliminated but, as a reality, is inseparable from the reality which constitutes the universe. He would understand the pointlessness of the suicidal act. (How can I, who exist, enter a realm of nothingness? Nothingness would have to be a reality to be a *real* nothingness.) It would teach him a reverence for reality, even, paradoxically, for his own thoughts of self-destruction, but without the desperate need to rid himself of them. He would understand that he needs no rescuing, especially not from anything real, being real himself. If he feels threatened, it is a mere appearance which it would be a mistake to take too seriously.

Thus the would-be suicide comes down from the bridge-rail and goes home, smiling to himself at a foolishness that would have prompted a melodramatic leap from a bridge, a flight from the productions of his own mind which are better fled by ceasing to produce them.

He had seen himself only as a *kind* of thing

and, as a result, as something, unique and different. This point of view had been a comfort to his ego. With such a consciousness, unconditioned by any deeper perception of his radical unseparateness as a being from the ground of being itself, he had always been on guard to protect his "interests," to assert his rights and prerogatives, to keep from being swept away by other more powerful kinds of things. He formed associations with his kind of thing, first with humans, then with people of *his* race, *his* religion, *his* nationality, *his* profession. There were definite advantages to this "kind-of-thing" approach to reality, but some obvious disadvantages, too. He was always outnumbered, always in danger of being swamped by so many other kinds of things. There was only one remedy for the problem, namely, that of associating himself with things *insofar as they are real*, with that characteristic everything has, namely, reality. With such an affiliation he would never be in the minority, never be threatened, never have to be an aggressor in order to maintain himself.

Clearly, so long as the human mind is only used to perceive kinds of things, consciousness can have no avenue to a vision of a universe cohering in being. The universe will appear rather as fragmented, consisting of a multiplicity of selves, all isolated and competitive. One then fights as long as one can and when the battle is clearly lost to the "other selves," one does not struggle on in torment—one capitulates; one jumps off a bridge.

On its face, the proposal that there is only one universal Self will meet great resistance. Common sense finds it preposterous and the physical sciences would rule it unverified (and unverifiable), a useless metaphysical abstraction. Hindu thinkers, it is true, would have no difficulty accepting the reality of a universal Self, but most other theological experts would vigorously reject the proposal for a variety of reasons, Christian, Jews and Moslems as pantheistic, Buddhists as theistic.

Yet there is a single, important strain in Christian metaphysics that would be hospitable to the notion of a single universal Self. This strain is underground and elitist, and is ignored by theological orthodoxy rather than directly challenged. It originated with St. Thomas Aquinas. Aquinas spent his relatively short life of forty-nine years building a sound, earth-escaping "missile system" (he was the missile) which he launched shortly before he died, sending back the message that his writings were "straw" compared to what he experienced mystically. Later, one of his close students, the celebrated Meister Eckhart, was to use Aquinas' launching system for his own mystical journeyings (proving it was not some idiosyncratic system and that straw can sometimes be used to remarkable purpose).

What was it, then, that St. Thomas Aquinas held on the subject of the nature of reality viewed in terms of its being? His words, exactly translated from the Latin, are as follows: *"Being, however, insofar as it is being, cannot be diverse."*[6]

Astonishing as it may sound, the master theologian-philosopher of Christendom taught a doctrine which, while never couched in the classical Hindu idiom of the single Self, is compatible with that idiom. For when you hold, as Aquinas clearly did, that the existence of creatures is not other than the very existence of God, you are in fact affirming what the Hindus explicitly affirm on the subject, namely, that "Brahman alone pervades everything above and below; this universe is that Supreme Brahman alone."[7]

> The swami asked me to stand up. I followed him to another, much smaller platform which I had not seen before. Here was a small pyre of wood, not yet alight. I was asked to lie on it. The swami approached me with a firebrand and some live charcoal. He touched my body in seven places. Symbolically, the pyre was set on fire. Symbolically, I was now being cremated. As I stood up, I made my own obsequial rite, with the *mantras* which are chanted by the living for the dead. It signifies when the sannyasi (the ordained Hindu monk) says "I," he does not mean his body, not his senses, not his mind, not his intellect. "I" means the cosmic spirit, the Brahman, and it is with This that he henceforth identifies himself. This is the only important difference between the monk and the layman. The layman too is Brah-

man, and so is all that lives. The monk is Brahman too, but the monk is aware of it, the sannyasi
is aware of nothing else. Or at least, he should be
aware of nothing else.[8]

And so we return to the suicide on the
bridge. He is soon to discover that there is but
one Self. It is not other than the uncreated existence within him. It will survive the fall, as it
does every calamity, every annihilation of worlds.
It is the eternal Self of the universe.

We have spent a whole book learning how to
protect the self, nourish it, govern it, inform it,
etc. All before we properly found it. There was a
reason for this, a reason which, if the reader were
the writer (who can *really* distinguish us?), he or
she would surely understand. The reason is this:
*There is no self (in the sense of a separate ego) to
find or rescue in the first place.*

> *One went to the door of the Beloved and*
>   *knocked.*
> *A voice asked, "Who is there?"*
> *He answered, "It is I."*
> *The voice said, "There is no room for Me and*
>   *Thee."*
> *The door was shut.*
> *After a year of solitude and deprivation he re-*
>   *turned and knocked.*
> *A voice from within asked, "Who is there?"*
> *The man said, "It is Thee."*
> *The door was opened for him.*[9]

Epilogue—
Reality Dialogue

Vocatus atque non vocatus, Deus aderit.
(Called or not called, God is present).

INSCRIPTION ON THE GATE AT THE HOME OF
C.G. JUNG IN KUSNACHT, SWITZERLAND

1 *What is real?*
That which is more than nothing.

2 *Are some things more real than others?*
Surely. Things are more real than thoughts.

3 *How do you know?*
Well, for one thing, thoughts only become real
when and if you think them. Things are real
whether you think about them or not. Think of
what you mean by tree. The meaning of a large,

growing plant with roots, a trunk and branches actually exists *as a thought* only when you, or someone else, are actively thinking it. Stop thinking the thought and the thought doesn't exist anymore; it loses the reality you gave it when you thought it.

5 *Okay, but why are things more real than thoughts?*
Because anything which is independent of our thinking is more real than that which depends upon thinking for its very reality. Dreams are real only when we dream them and, consequently, less real than the waking world. Yet, even dreams are real since they are more than merely nothing. They seem very real during the dream, but when we wake up we realize they were, as we say, "only a dream."

6 *But how does thinking make thoughts real?*
In the first place, by being real itself. The thinking of imaginary men presumably cannot produce real thoughts. Being real itself, thinking is able to produce creatures like unto itself, namely, thoughts.

All mental states gain their reality from mental acts: no thinking, no thoughts; no imagining, no images; no ideologizing, no ideas; no conceptualizing, no concepts. Thoughts and images seem real because they *are* real; the heroine being strangled on the movie screen *is* real to the viewer who lives through a real concern for her safety and well-being. Yet, with it all, the actress is not *really* being strangled. In all this tangle of experience, the thoughts and images are *really* only thoughts and images. Which is to say that thoughts and images are a different kind of reality than things. This means, of course, that the passionate involvement with the fate of the heroine is, really speaking, a passionate involvement with the fate of images and/or ideas. One's excitement at the picture house is "much ado about nothing," to quote Shakespeare. More accurately, much ado about fictions of the mind.

7 *Well then, how do things become real? They are not thoughts, and yet they are real.*
In the same way that thoughts become real, namely, by being produced by a previously real reality. A look at the reality of the novel may shed some light. Consider the characters in the novel *Robinson Crusoe.* As you read the book, in your mind's eye you see Crusoe, that lonely shipwrecked man, adjusted to his desert home, strolling on the beach, his goat-umbrella in hand. He returns to his stockade and social-izes with his parrot, his dog, his cat. Friday enters and Crusoe, using the language he has taught his man, says, "Friday, do you suppose we are real?" Friday is obliging, but no help.

He is not able to say. What does he know, after all, of the "outside" order of the mind of Daniel Defoe, of the author who one day took up pen in hand and brought him and his master and island into being? Clearly, Friday could say nothing about this "outside order," unless he was given the power to say it by Defoe. But, in reading the book, if we chanced upon just such metaphysical words as "Nobody produced us, we just are, Mr. Crusoe," we would smile at the obvious contradiction such words imply. We would know at once that Friday is mistaken and the "cause" of his mistake can only be Daniel Defoe.

8 *Are you saying God produces things? I don't believe in God.*
"God" is a word which has regrettably lost its original meaning in our language.

9 *All right, then, what is the original meaning of the word "God"?*
It meant originally (and should still mean) "the being who simply exists."

10 *Where did this meaning originate?*
One of the places is in the Old Testament (Exod. 3:14).

11 *In which I do not believe, so we are at an impasse.*
Only if the meaning is in some way self-contradictory. Let's see if it is.

12 *I am willing to listen, though it's an effort.*
Someone who doesn't believe that God spoke
in the Old Testament, revealing his nature as
existence, might still have a speculative interest in exploring its logic. After all, the Pythagorean theorem doesn't exist anywhere in nature, yet we study it in geometry.

13 *Yet, the square of the hypotenuse does equal*
the sum of the squares of the opposite sides.
That I know. I don't have merely to believe in
it.
That's because you have studied geometry
and have been through the proof of that particular theorem. A lot of people have not, and all
they are able to do is believe that it is true. Actually, the theorem remains true, you will notice, whether one apprehends it by knowledge
or by belief. Thus the man who knows the
truth of the theorem is not at an impasse with
one who merely believes it, or even with one
who does not believe it even though it is true.
Not a genuine impasse.

14 *What do you mean by a genuine impasse?*
I mean a case in which one believes, for example, that the square of the hypotenuse is
not equal to the sum of the square of the other
two sides and tries to demonstrate it as true to
another similar believer.

15 *Is that what you mean by self-contradictory?*
It is. If the Pythagorean theorem is true, then

any variation in the formulation of it would be a contradiction of it and be false. The erroneous formulation would contradict itself.

16 *Let's get back to God as existence itself. I don't believe it, and I surely don't know it.*
First let's finish with Pythagoras. I said earlier that thoughts were not things. Do you agree?

17 *I do. But so what?*
Because I want you to decide right now in what class of reality the Pythagorean theorem is: Is it a thought or a thing?

18 *I'm not sure.*
Fair enough. Let me ask you this: Is there such a *thing* as a circle? I mean a real circular thing equidistant at every point of its circumference from its center?

19 *Are you trying to tell me that circles don't exist?*
Not at all. They most certainly do exist. But *where* is most important. They exist only in the mind, as a thought. And the same is true of the Pythagorean theorem.

20 *What are you driving at? I don't see the connection with God.*
What I am driving at is this: Since the Pythagorean theorem is not self-contradictory, it is true to say that if, I repeat the *if*, a right triangle ever existed the way, say, apples do, it

would have to have the nature described by the Pythagorean theorem. The same is true exactly of God. If He exists, He has to have the nature described in the Old Testament; i.e., if He exists at all, it must be as existence itself.

21 *I'm afraid that I do not see the need for this necessity even viewed hypothetically.*
That may be because you think there is something more important than existence.

22 *Such as?*
Well, motion, goodness, unity, etc.

23 *I'm afraid you lost me.*
Well, in physics you were taught that if a material thing became atomically motionless, it would cease to be. This suggests that motion is more fundamental than existence, although in fact it implies just the reverse.

24 *How does it imply that existence is more fundamental than motion in this particular case?*
Because it would cease to *be* if it lost all atomic motion. This implies the prior importance of existence.

25 *Yes, but in this case, at least, motion causes it to be.*
Not so.

26 *Why not so?*
For a very good reason that goes back to some earlier discussion. Motion is like a circle, it

has only a mental reality. There are cars moving on the highway, but you will never see motion, just plain motion, moving on the highway. And since motion is a mental reality, it does not *cause* moving things to move. Any more than human thought causes the world of real things to exist. Yet motion is not nothing. It is a real idea. A moving car is a real *thing*. Notice how the whole problem hinges on the question of reality. We might point out here that Newton's Law of Inertia, that a body in motion continues in motion in a straight line until acted upon by an imbalanced force needs the metaphysical qualifier, *provided it continues to exist*, to be a fully scientific law.

27 *Something has to be before it can move. I'll buy that. But what causes it to be?*
That depends on what you are talking about. Some real beings (thoughts) are caused to be by real thinking, as remarked earlier. Other real beings (sensible things, like cars and apples) are much more difficult to account for causally, except to say that there are only two possibilities, namely, (1) they cause their own being, or (2) they are caused by a previously existing reality.

28 *How about a third possibility, namely, they were caused by nothing?*
Do you mean by a nothing lacking all reality?

29 *Yes. Pure nothing. No reality at all.*
How can nothing have any causal power?

30 *Simple. The void is nothing, and yet it is necessary to have it before you can fill it. Try filling something that is already full.*
Try filling the void with another void. I'm afraid when you add nothing to nothing you get precisely nothing. Nothing is caused or produced.

31 *I'm not denying that something has causal power; I'm simply saying that nothing has causal power, too.*
Causal power to do what?

32 *To receive something. In this respect, it is actually more powerful than something. Try putting something into a place already occupied by something. You get a collision.*
I'll be the first to admit that something is not an improvement on something, only on nothing. Or perhaps I should say that if you are in a place already, I could never find you somewhere else for purposes of improving on you where you are. In other words, I am saying that if what exists is all it could be, then nothing would have no role to play at all. Reality would be a total causality, driving out nothing completely. With such a totality, there would be no nothingness to be filled, and no

causality of any kind whatever to be exercised by it.

33 *What strikes me is that with such a totality of being as you describe, all causality would come to an end.*
In a sense you are perfectly right. I have never been happy with the description of God as the uncaused cause, because of its self-contradiction. And yet it does bring out your point about where the logic of total existence leads, namely, to the death of the very possibility of the causality. But, also, to the impossibility of that third possibility you just referred to, nothingness as a cause.

34 *I'm not ready to give up on that possibility. If I did, nothing new could happen, including even this conversation. I mean this very conversation—its sounds, its words, its ideas, its truth—is not "bumping into" something already there which is identical with it, the way in which I am identical with myself. You are not trying to maintain that, surely, are you? And if you are not, then nothingness is being filled and, furthermore, making its own, no doubt poor, but indispensable contribution to the operation.*
In the absolute sense, I am forced to say that nothing new is ever really happening. Which is to say that all events are really happening

within the divine "mind," in the unchanging God.

35 *What do you mean by "in the absolute sense"? Perhaps that is the sticking point of this whole controversy and a satisfactory answer to this question will end it, if you can come up with one, which I doubt.*

The existence of everything is included in the divine existence. This means that absolutely everything is God.[1] Nothingness, therefore, is merely the unsuccessful attempt by the human brain to contain or to finite-ize the divine reality. This attempt is called "human-thought-when-thought-of-as-*something*-by-the-human-mind." Such thinking is the "death" of God. It is also the death of other living things, as well. Atomic death is inevitable for a universe which has been atomized by human thought.

36 *Would this ultimately mean the end of all existence?*

No. Existence, which is God, cannot end. Or even be threatened with an ending. God's only "enemy" is nothingness. Or, to put it another way, the only enemy of God cannot even be conceived by Himself.

A Self Rescue Exercise

On the path.
Pick up the foot,
Put it down:
Pick it up, put it down.
Try it.
Try picking up the foot
And putting it down.
Only that.
Only the foot being raised,
Thrust ahead.
Put down.
Only that.
Child's play for a Sayadaw.*
For you,
For me,
Thought:
Plans, dreams, concerns, intimidations, circum-
    stances,

213

Intentions, doubts, regrets, expectations, propos-
als,
Schemes, worries, excitements, agonies, ambi-
tions,
Feelings, arguments, contradictions, crises, joys,
Plots, hints, quarrels, conquests, conditions,
Insults, motives, mistakes, maneuvers, affections,
Mystifications, envies, fantasies, qualifications,
laments. . . .
The foot on the path:
Pick it up, put it down.
Child's play?
Burmese tricks?
Try it.
Try it.

*For a fascinating account of the Sayadaw and Satipatthana medita-
tion, see the book by the British Admiral E. H. Shattock, *An Experiment in Mindfulness*, Samuel Weisner, New York, 1958.

Reference Notes

CHAPTER 2: How to Survive a Tragedy

1 William Shakespeare, *Hamlet*, act 4, scene 5.
2 William Shakespeare, *Sonnet 50.*
3 William Shakespeare, *King John*, act 3, scene 4, line 93.
4 William Shakespeare, *King Lear*, act 5, scene 3, line 307.

CHAPTER 4: How to Live with Remorse

1 Emily Dickinson, Poem 670, *The Complete Poems of Emily Dickinson*, edited by Thomas H. Johnson (Boston: Little, Brown, 1960), p. 333.
2 Edward Fitzgerald, *The Rubaiyat of Omar Khayyam*, stanza 71.
3 John Greenleaf Whittier, "Maud Muller," stanza 53.

CHAPTER 6: How to Cure an Ulcer

1 William Butler Yeats, "Blood and the Moon," *Collected Poems* (New York: Macmillan, 1964), p. 233.

2 Dorothy Donath, *Buddhism for the West* (New York: Julian Press, 1971), p. 134.

CHAPTER 8: How to Do What You Really Want to Do

1 Dr. Wilder Penfield, *The Mystery of the Mind* (Princeton, N.J.: Princeton University Press, 1975), pp. 61–62.

CHAPTER 9: How to Keep a Promise

1 See Gregory Bateson, with D. D. Jackson, J. Haley and J. H. Weakland, "Toward a Theory of Schizophrenia," *Behavioral Science*, vol. 1 (Oct. 4, 1956), pp. 251–264. An example of the "double-bind" effect is as follows: a wife complains to her husband that he never tells her that he loves her. He then does so and is told, "You're only saying that because I complained," clearly a no-win dilemma for the husband.
2 A. N. Whitehead has pointed out that the moral order of the universe consists in the fact that evil is self-stultifying.
3 Swami Prabhavananda and Christopher Isherwood (eds.), *How to Know God* (New York: Mentor Books, 1969), p. 103.

CHAPTER 13: How to Zero In on Reality

1 Quoted by D. T. Suzuki in *Mysticism: Christian and Buddhist* (New York: Collier Books, 1962), p. 64.
2 Bashō, *The Narrow Road to the Deep North and Other Travel Sketches* (Baltimore: Penguin, 1966), p. 131.
3 *Ibid.*, p. 129.
4 *Ibid.*, p. 123.
5 *Ibid.*, p. 33.
6 Robert Louis Stevenson, "On Respectability."

7 T. S. Eliot, "Burnt Norton," *Four Quartets, The Complete Poems and Plays* (New York: Harcourt, Brace & World, 1971), p. 120.

8 William Carlos Williams, "The Red Wheelbarrow," *Selected Poems* (New York: New Directions, 1969), p. 30.

CHAPTER 14: How to Forget the Past

1 Michael Crichton, *Terminal Man* (New York: Alfred Knopf, 1972), p. 233.

CHAPTER 17: How to Tune in to Things

1 Lama Anagarika Govinda, *Foundations of Tibetan Mysticism* (New York: Dutton, 1960), p. 47.

2 Idries Shah, *The Sufis* (New York: Anchor Books, 1971), pp. 413–414.

3 A Monk of the Eastern Church, *The Prayer of Jesus* (New York: Desclee, 1967), p. 11.

4 *Letter to the Philippians,* 2:9–10.

5 Lama Govinda, *op. cit.,* p. 19. "Thus, the word in the hour of its birth was a centre of force and reality, and only habit has stereotyped it into a mere conventional medium of expression. The mantra escaped this fate to a certain extent, because it had no concrete meaning and could therefore not be made to subserve utilitarian ends."

6 Prabhavananda and Isherwood (eds.), *op. cit.,* p. 43.

7 *Ibid.,* p. 41.

CHAPTER 18: How to Be Cheerful

1 E. E. Cummings, *Selected Letters* (New York: Harcourt, Brace and World, 1969), p. 271.

CHAPTER 19: How to Be Brave

1 William Shakespeare, *Macbeth,* act 5, scene 3.

2 That which is dealt with dishonestly imposes penalties. In the case of death, one penalty is in having to support the costly, inept and even harmful attitudes and practices which Jessica Mitford writes about in her book *The American Way of Death*. The sorrow of loss which modern Western funeral customs are designed to deal with is, in large measure, induced sorrow, sorrow created by a materialized culture more than by genuine natural instincts. It is a sorrow which is "good for business," while it pretends to be good for the bereaved. Expressions of sorrow and grief are manifestations of solidarity with the particular culture, as the differences in reaction to death, ranging from the suicidal suttee of the Hindu widow to the marry-the-next-day insouciance of the Western sophisticate, make clear.

3 See Elizabeth Kubler-Ross, *On Death and Dying* (New York: Macmillan 1969), and her other writings. See also Dr. Raymond A. Moody, Jr., *Life after Life* (New York: Bantam, 1976).

4 William Blake, "Proverbs," line 5.

5 Alan Watts, *Beyond Theology* (New York: Pantheon Books, 1964), p. 228.

6 Gerard Manley Hopkins, "God's Grandeur."

7 G. K. Chesterton, "The Skeleton," *The Collected Poems* (New York: Dodd, Mead & Company, 1930), p. 305.

CHAPTER 20: How to Find Yourself

1 Prabhavananda and Isherwood (eds.), *op. cit.*, p. 135.

2 *Ibid.*, p. 148.

3 *Chandogya Upanishad*, verse 13.

4 Al Ghazzali, *Mishkat Al-Answar*, p. 64. See also Chapter 112 of the *Koran*.

5 The Epistle of St. John, 7:21.

6 *Summa Contra Gentiles*, II, 52. *"Esse autem in quantum est esse non potest esse diversum."* On this point two distinguished commentators on St. Thomas have written as follows: "Beings (entia) are diverse, but not *esse*; nor are beings diverse by reason of their *esse*." Rev. Gerald Phelan, "The Being of Creatures," *Selected Papers* (Toronto: Pontifical Institute of Mediaeval Studies, 1967), p. 89.
"There is but one nature of being. It includes in itself the totality of being. That nature is not increased nor extended in any way by the production of other things. A million galaxies mean hundreds of millions of beings in the universe. But they do not mean the least bit more being than there was before anything was caused, or than there would be if they were nonexistent." Rev. Joseph Owens, C.S.s.R., *An Elementary Christian Metaphysics* (Milwaukee: Bruce, 1963), p. 108.
7 *The Mundaha Upanishad*, II, ii, 2.
8 Agehananda Bharati, *The Ochre Robe* (New York: Anchor Books, 1970), pp. 153–154.
9 Jalaluddin Rumi, quoted by Idries Shah, *The Sufis* (New York: Anchor Books, 1971).

EPILOGUE

1 The way a Christian philosopher might express his pantheism without giving offense is by saying "God is everything" rather than "Everything is God." It is not my intention here to scandalize. In fact, I do not look at a creature, a human, a worm, whatever, and see God with my eyes. I simply hold that the *existence* of creatures *is*, indeed must be, the very existence of God—while maintaining philosophically the real distinction between *what* a creature is (its essence) and *that* it is (its existence).

Suggested Reading

BHARATI, Agehananda. *The Ochre Robe*. New York: Doubleday, 1970.

BLOFELD, John. *The Wheel of Life*. San Francisco: Shambala, 1972.

_____. *The Secret and the Sublime*. New York: Dutton, 1973.

BROWN, Spencer G. *Laws of Form*. London: Allen & Unwin, 1969.

BUBER, Martin. *Good and Evil*. New York: Scribners, 1953.

CAMPBELL, Joseph. *The Hero with a Thousand Faces*. New York: World, 1967.

CARLO, William E. *Philosophy, Science and Knowledge*. Milwaukee: Bruce, 1967.

_____. *The Ultimate Reducibility of Essence to Existence*. The Hague: Martinus Nijhoff, 1967.

COOMARASWAMY, Ananda. *Buddha and the Gospel of Buddhism*. New York: Asia Publishing House, 1956.

DECHANET, J.M. *Christian Yoga*. New York: Desclee, 1960.

ELIADE, Mircea. *Yoga: Immortality and Freedom*. Princeton, NJ: Bollingen, 1969.

FRANKL, Viktor E. *The Doctor and the Soul*. New York: Alfred Knopf, 1955.

GILSON, Etienne. *Being and Some Philosophers*. Toronto: Pontifical Institute of Mediaeval Studies, 1952.

GOVINDA, Anagarika Lama. *Foundations of Tibetan Mysticism*. New York: Dutton, 1960.

_____. *The Way of the White Clouds*. London: Hutchinson, 1966.

GRAHAM, Aelred Dom. *Conversations: Christian and Buddhist*. New York: Harcourt, Brace & World, 1968.

HERRIGEL, Eugene. *Zen in the Art of Archery*. New York: Pantheon, 1959.

JOURARD, Sidney M. *The Transparent Self.* New York: Van Nostrand, 1968.

KAPLEAU, Philip. *The Three Pillars of Zen.* New York: Harper & Row, 1966.

KILEY, John Cantwell. *Equilibrium.* Los Angeles: Guild of Tutors Press, 1980.

_____. *Einstein and Aquinas.* The Hague: Martinus Nijhoff, 1969.

MARITAIN, Jacques. *Existence and The Existent.* New York: Pantheon, 1948.

MASLOW, Abraham. *Toward a Psychology of Being.* New York: Van Nostrand, 1968.

MERTON, Thomas. *The Way of Chuang Tzu.* New York: New Directions, 1965.

_____. *Zen and the Birds of Appetite.* New York: New Directions, 1968.

A Monk of the Eastern Church. *The Prayer of Jesus.* New York: Desclee, 1967.

OTTO, Rudolph. *Mysticism East and West.* New York: Meridian, 1960.

OWENS, Joseph. *An Elementary Christian Metaphysics.* Milwaukee: Bruce, 1963.

PATANJALI. *How to Know God.* Edited by Swami Phabhavananda and Christopher Isherwood. New York: Mentor, 1953.

PIERRE, Joseph H. Jr. *The Road to Damascus.* New York: Irvington Publisher, 1981.

PHELAN, Gerald. *Selected Papers.* Toronto: Pontifical Institute of Mediaeval Studies, 1967.

ROSS, Nancy Wilson. *The World of Zen.* New York: Random House, 1960.

ST. THOMAS AQUINAS. *On Being and Essence.* Edited by A. Maurer. Toronto: Pontifical Institute of Mediaeval Studies, 1968.

SHAH, Idres. *The Sufis.* New York: Anchor Books, 1971.

SHATTOCK, E.H. *An Experiment in Mindfulness.* New York: Samuel Weiser, 1958.

222

UNDERHILL, Evelyn. *Mysticism*. New York: New American Library, 1955.

WATTS, Alan. *The Way of Zen*. New York: Pantheon, 1957.

_____. *The Two Hands of God*. New York: George Braziller, 1963.

_____. *Beyond Theology*. New York: Pantheon, 1964.

_____. *The Book: On the Taboo Against Knowing Who You Are*. New York: Pantheon, 1966.

_____. *In My Own Way*. New York: Pantheon, 1972.

WEIL, Andrew. *The Natural Mind*. New York: Houghton Mifflin, 1972.

WHITROW, G.J. *The Nature of Time*. New York: Holt, Rinehart & Winston, 1972.

ZIMMER, Heinrich. *Myths and Symbols in Indian Art and Civilization*. New York: Harper, 1946.

About the Author

John Cantwell Kiley is among the very few therapists trained both in medicine and in philosophy. There are, he insists, properly philosophical diseases, and in *Self Rescue,* he stakes out a domain which has, as it were, "fallen between the cracks." This domain, though theoretically within the "visible spectrum" of human suffering, and though very real to the sufferer, is seen best—and often only—by a philosopher. Ideally the philosopher/therapist has sufficient medical and psychological training to rule out kidney disease or personality disorders.

INDEX OF NAMES

INDEX OF SUBJECTS